BECOMING A SUCCESSFUL INTRAPRENEUR

A practical guide to creating an innovative information service

Sheila Pantry OBE and Peter Griffiths

LIBRARY ASSOCIATION PUBLISHING
LONDON

© Sheila Pantry and Peter Griffiths 1998

Published by
Library Association Publishing
7 Ridgmount Street
London WC1E 7AE

Library Association Publishing is wholly owned by The Library Association.

First published 1998

British Library Cataloguing in Publication Data
A catalogue record for this book is available from the British Library.

ISBN 1-85604-292-8

Typeset in 11/14 pt Aldine 721 by Library Association Publishing.
Printed and made in Great Britain by Bookcraft (Bath) Ltd, Midsomer Norton, Somerset.

BECOMING A SUCCESSFUL INTRAPRENEUR

A practical guide to creating an innovative information service

Other titles in the Successful LIS Professional series

Liz MacLachlan   Making project management work for you

Ailsa Masterton   Getting results with time management

Beryl Morris   First steps in management

Tim Owen   Success at the enquiry desk

Sheila Pantry   Dealing with aggression and violence in your workplace

John Kirby et al.   Empowering the information user

Contents

Series Editor's preface vii

Foreword ix

1   Introducing the information intrapreneur 1
          Information and society 1
          What are intrapreneurs? 3
          The information intrapreneur 4
          A revolution in information and library services 6
          Making a mark in the organization 7
          Intrapreneurs at large 7
          Characteristics of the intrapreneur 8

2   The organization and the information intrapreneur 12
          What is the 'organization'? 12
          Organizational publications 13
          People within the organization 14
          Library-derived information 16
          What sort of information is used – and what is it used for? 17
          How the information professional squares up to knowledge management 18

3   The internal information audit 22
          Information audit 23
          Undecided management 24
          Defining information resources and services 24
          The objective of the audit 28
          Underlying issues for the information auditor 29

4   Keeping one step ahead of the customers 35
          Why it is essential that the information staff keep up-to-date 35
          Customers' expectations 36
          Giving the answers before the questions are asked 36
          Further ways of keeping ahead 38
          Quality management 39
          Communicating the information message 40

Learning how to market the information service   42
Critical success factors (CSFs)   43
How to stay ahead   43

5   Delivering innovative services   45
New technology   45
Providing access   46
Imaginative use of the technology   47
Enhancing access   49
Practical problems in developing services   51
Core skills   52
New partnerships   52
Turning information into a value added service   53

6   Building the perfect team   54
Why the team is so important   54
Skills and knowledge   55
Managing the intrapreneurial team   57
Team playing beyond the information and library service   58

7   Setting and maintaining standards   61
Why standards are needed   61
How service level agreements help   63
Putting yourself in the customer's chair   66
Quality and performance management   67
Obtaining user feedback   68

8   Marketing and promotion   70
Image   71
Communication   72
Defining the marketing plan   73
The publicity vehicles to be used   75
The budget allocation   77
Evaluation of the success of the marketing plan and publicity   77

Appendix 1 Sample audit forms   79

Appendix 2 Further reading   89

Index   97

Series Editor's preface

With rapid technological advances and new freedoms, the workplace presents a dynamic and challenging environment. It is just these advances, however, that necessitate a versatile and adaptable workforce that knows that lifelong full-time jobs are a thing of the past. Work is being contracted out, de-structured organizations are emerging, and different skills and approaches are required from 'brain-workers' who must solve new and changing problems. All workers must become self-motivated, multi-skilled and constantly learning. Demonstrating the international economic importance of professional development, the European Commission has officially voiced its commitment to a European community committed to lifelong learning.

For the information professional, the key to success in this potentially destabilizing context is to develop the new skills the workplace demands. Above all, the LIS professional must actively prioritize a commitment to continuous professional development. The information industry is growing fast and the LIS profession is experiencing very rapid change. This series has been designed to help you manage change by prioritizing the growth of your own portfolio of professional skills. By reading these books you will have begun the process of seeing yourself as your own best resource and begun the rewarding challenge of staying ahead of the game.

The series is a very practical one, focusing on specific topics relevant to all types of library and information service. Recognizing that your time is precious, these books have been written so that they may be easily read and digested. They include instantly applicable ideas and techniques which you can put to the test in your own workplace, helping you to succeed in your job.

The authors have been selected because of their practical experience and enthusiasm for their chosen topic and we hope you will benefit from their advice and guidance. The points for reflection, checklists and summaries are designed to provide stepping stones for you to assess your understanding of the topic as you read.

This book will help you succeed in making your information service even more dynamic. It will help you identify the many opportunities to use your skills and ideas that will truly make your information service central to your organization. Only by constantly keeping in touch with your customers will you really know what type of information and information services they require. There are so many ways, including the use of the technologies that you can employ, to provide that perfect information service.

Peter Griffiths and I draw on our respective experiences working in a variety of information services, from public libraries, private industries, nationalized organizations, to government service.

We wish you enjoyment and satisfaction as you become the most successful intrapreneur!

Sheila Pantry OBE

Foreword

Why this book?

Until recently libraries have been thought of as traditional, even stuffy, places and despite the efforts of professional bodies in many countries, the old-fashioned images have prevailed in the public mind.

Suddenly all this has changed. The rapid explosion of information media, in particular the World Wide Web, has taken public perceptions of information – and of the libraries where it is found – rapidly forward. However, expectations that all the information problems of people and organizations would be instantly solved by a simple search of the Web proved to be remarkably short-lived. Public awareness of information availability was quickly matched by frustration, first at the slowness of access and then, as the Web mushroomed in size, by annoyance at the difficulty of finding accurate information and the dismal organization of many websites.

Then the unexpected happened. Management gurus realized that one group of professionals knew all along what needed to be done – and they named this group. They were the librarians – who always were the true information professionals. Senior managers read the management literature and realized the importance of the resource they already employed. Communities struggling to make sense of the new means of electronic communication came to realize that their libraries could be not only a useful meeting place on winter evenings but also the centre for support in dealing with the new information age. And so on.

Unfortunately, some librarians have been slow to realize what is happening and to grasp the opportunities that have arrived. Their behaviour remains as it was before, reacting to events rather than leading them, and providing traditional services that could, frankly, have been provided even had much of the technology of the 20th century not been invented. This is dangerous behaviour, because others have observed the vital role that librarians can play and, should the librarians decline to take the initiative, are poised to do it in their stead (or worse still foul it up).

Nothing less than a new style of librarianship and information work can meet these challenges. We recognize that operating a private, profitable library as an independent contractor is (sadly) not yet possible. Accordingly we propose a style of entrepreneurial behaviour within companies, public sector organizations, and academic and local communities that recognizes the need for a supporting organization, but takes as many considered risks and initiatives as necessary to get the job done to the customer's satisfaction and delight, and addresses the real information needs of the users. This is the work of the library and information intrapreneur.

Looking at management practice, and considering current trends in information and library work such as knowledge management, we examine ways in which any information and library professional can develop an intrapreneurial style. Using case studies we suggest some possible avenues for intrapreneurial development, and provide worksheets for important processes such as information audits.

This book is designed to provide the successful information and library professional with both a source of ideas and a workbook for the new, intrapreneurial style of professional work.

Chapter 1
Introducing the information intrapreneur

In this chapter you will discover:

➤ the importance of information
➤ the characteristics of entrepreneurs
➤ the concept of the intrapreneur
➤ why the management of information and library services demands intrapreneurial behaviour in order to succeed.

Information and society

Information has achieved a high profile in modern society. People in all walks of life are familiar with the constant flow of information from newspapers, a multitude of television and radio channels, through a panoply of personal electronic devices such as pagers and handheld computers, to the information kiosks that we are promised as an imminent and everyday feature of our lives. Information is an issue on national political agendas. In the UK 'government.direct', the Major administration's prospectus for electronic government set out that government's view of what was possible and aimed to start a debate on the uses of information and information technology in support of the delivery of public services. Its offshoot information service 'direct.access.government' provides a range of government forms and documents. 'Better Government', the Blair administration's plans for further progress, again will concentrate heavily not only on technology but on the information content of electronic services to be created during its time in office. In the European Union (the Bangemann report) and its individual countries such as the Republic of Ireland (the Information Town project),

France (the Martin-Lalande and 'information society' reports), and Norway ('Bit by Bit') have followed similar themes. IT2000 in Singapore and the South Korean National Information Infrastructure project are just two of a range of initiatives that will affect the role of information and library professionals. And the Internet has not only made everyone aware of the information society, it has made everyone an expert on information retrieval – 'the answer is out there somewhere'.

The impact of technology

The technology of information – which is too often confused with the information itself – brings another round of opportunities. The use of electronic mail as a means of correspondence within and between organizations, the range of electronic databases and information resources, and the ability to edit and transform downloaded data to suit individual customers are all examples of services that have recently become widely accepted.

This technology offers the innovative library and information professional a range of ways to deliver a personalized service to customers: ways that are far removed from early efforts with thermal paper, scissors, glue and a photocopier.

But at the same time, people who deal in information, and who have been talking about the potential of an information revolution, have a considerable difficulty. Library and information professionals have an image problem.

This is not news, but colours both the way in which all kinds of organization consider their information and library services and the public perception of the librarian. In this book we shall be looking at various ways in which library and information professionals can – and should – demonstrate to their organizations and to the public, through a combination of marketing, corporate intelligence, management skills and innovative thought, that their function is not merely useful but essential at the start of the new millennium.

Information flow

Information is the lifeblood of any organization, and the library and information professional is vital to the understanding, exploitation and productive use of that information. In companies and public sector organizations, the importance of information must be taken to the corporate agenda and new approaches be used to highlight the contribution made by the library and information professional. In public libraries this means demonstrating the wide-ranging and often surprising contribution that the library makes to the community in return for its financial support. In the wider public domain, a growing wealth of information is available to the citizen through a wide range of media. Skilled intermediaries are required to act as facilitators or trainers, even if the ultimate aim is that people should be able to access information directly through public terminals in future. And in the academic sector, library and information professionals can show that their contribution helps the entire organization to move forward, both in terms of its management and in terms of its learning and research functions.

New skills and new areas of work, such as knowledge management, provide opportunities for lateral-thinking and innovative library and information professionals to demonstrate the value of both their skills and their thinking. A number of other professions are staking their claims to these areas of work, and the new technologies are blurring the boundaries. But we firmly believe that library and information professionals are best equipped to make sense of these new areas, and in this book we examine ways in which this could be done.

The key lies in a new style of management, which is described as intrapreneurial, and its application to information and library service management.

What are intrapreneurs?

First of all, what exactly do we mean by 'intrapreneur'? You may imagine that intrapreneurs are a relatively recent breed of worker, though the term is based on the word 'entrepreneur', which itself is rather older than perhaps might be thought. It dates back at least to the writer Richard Cantillon who used it in 1734 to describe someone who bought cheap and sold dear. By 1800, the French economist J. B. Say had expanded the definition to someone who moves economic resources into an area of higher productivity and greater yield. In time the meaning has widened to denote a freewheeling and dynamic style of business management, often based on personal style and risk.

We first hear of intrapreneurs in the 1980s, as more analysis was made of the rapid changes taking place in business and society, and it was realized that these characteristics existed not only in commercial and business environments but also within larger organizations. In the latter, whether they were in the public sector or large commercial bodies, some of those who wished to act as entrepreneurs were unable to do so because of the organization's structures around them. This might be because the body was publicly funded and therefore subject to particular accounting rules, or because it would be seen as commercial activity within a non-commercial environment (or indeed the inverse). But there would be no fundamental reason why people should not act as entrepreneurs, within the structure of their organizations, whilst complying with most or all of the rules of the body in which they are employed.

Other terms for intrapreneurship include 'civil entrepreneurship' and 'social entrepreneurship', both of which have been used in recent British publications. At the end of this chapter are details of characteristics of these civil or social entrepreneurs taken from surveys in the United Kingdom, and the references for this chapter include recent work on the public and charitable sectors.

The information intrapreneur

In this book, we focus on a particular type of intrapreneur, the information intrapreneur. Companies and public bodies spend millions of pounds annually on acquiring information in all shapes and forms. Much of it is bought in multiple copies, badly managed and ultimately abandoned or lost. When it is needed urgently, it may well be purchased a second time. Information is lost at an alarming rate, whilst inaccurate information replaces it from informal and formal resources, causing unnecessary expense and creating competitive disadvantage for organizations and possibly serious consequences for individuals.

The person with the combination of abilities to resolve these problems to the benefit of both the customer and the information and library service is the information (or library) intrapreneur. And it is the skills and training of the library and information professional that can resolve the problems and provide the ideal background for intrapreneurship.

Many library and information professionals are already familiar to some degree with this kind of operation, for example by having to market their services in an organization that does not otherwise carry out internal or external marketing, or by needing to take a wider view of their role in the organization in order to ensure survival during downsizing.

In the public sector, communities will often remark on the librarian's skills in networking for general benefit, but fail to exploit those same skills when other local projects are being undertaken. The tribal memory of a library service can for example unearth forgotten facts that will explain or confirm events taking place in a community in which many residents may be recent arrivals, or that may have existed as a large community only for a short time. The public library will in many cases be the only collective source of information for suburban communities that grew up early in the twentieth century and where its first residents are no longer able to provide anecdotal information about their histories. The community information networks maintained by librarians are often recognized as valuable, but viewed as passive tools to be constructed and then consulted almost as a last resort. The innovative library and information professional has the ability to make these resources into proactive tools.

In the academic sector the library and information professional also has a range of opportunities to move from being the guardian of a reactive store to managing a central and crucial resource for the organization. In an environment that is founded on research there will be little need to promote the scholarly aspects of the work of the library, but the contribution of information and of its professional managers may well need to be made clear at a managerial and organization-wide level.

A revolution in information and library services

For once there really is no time like the present in the information and library world. The rapid emergence of the Internet and its capture of the popular imagination have led to a new and widespread appreciation of the issues and problems of information management, such as access to a worldwide fund of information, its sheer size, the difficulty of navigating it, the conflicts of information within it. These issues of organizing information have become apparent to a wide public, including corporate managements, because now the popular media are describing them. (Library and information staff have been talking about them for years, but, sadly, unheeded.)

Recent plans to revolutionize library services in the UK have brought a new public awareness of the possibilities of information and the role of librarians in managing it. Government now recognizes the value of library and information professionals' skills, and has proposals to meet their development needs. The information and library service is an ideal place for the intrapreneurial spirit to flourish. Herbert S. White has pointed out that most organizations will not intervene in the operation of their library unless it appears that the library is about to bankrupt or otherwise severely embarrass the parent body. Most organizations take the view that the library is a necessary cost burden, and is managed by professionals who will act in a responsible, competent, but essentially unexciting way. This view results in a minimal degree of management, usually by a person with little understanding of information work, and a remarkably free hand for the head of the information and library service who nonetheless has responsibility for considerable amounts of money and resources.

In any other section of the organization, the degree of supervision and controls placed upon the information and library service would probably be considered inadequate. The reader of this book would be irresponsible to take advantage of this situation for his or her own ends, but such a degree of freedom is sufficient to allow a dynamic approach to information and library service development. The opportunity exists to add to job satisfaction whilst potentially bringing considerable benefit to the organization, and it is this opportunity and its potential which we shall be examining in detail in the remainder of this book.

Making a mark in the organization

The first part of the job of an information intrapreneur is to make sure that the organization (or community, or whatever) realizes that there is no viable alternative to a professional information and library service. (The non-viable alternative is to do without information – a strategy that works fine until the first blunder through lack of information, following which the problem may well disappear when the organization goes out of existence or the community splinters through lack of communication.)

The second part of the job is to ensure that the organization realizes that its information and library services are not simply a cost overhead, but can contribute to the bottom line of the balance sheet, certainly in terms of value added and perhaps in hard cash. If more money cannot be voted to the information and library service, then the service should at least show that it is providing more value for every pound, dollar or euro than it did before. An information and library service that can demonstrate this approach has the right to be heard, and respected for its contribution.

At the same time we might note some of the personality characteristics of the entrepreneur as identified in the literature. They have been seen as individuals who may be isolated within society; they may fit poorly with society, and may be spurred into entrepreneurial action by this. They may indeed be members of some minority. The personality traits of librarians have often been described similarly: it is now time for those librarians who fit this stereotype to develop its positive features.

Intrapreneurs at large

Much of the development of the concept of the intrapreneur has been the work of the writer Gifford Pinchot. He realized that not only is it possible for organizations to agree to a form of internal market and entrepreneurial behaviour, but that this could be a positive benefit. At the simplest level, the intrapreneur can be a person with an innovative idea who creates the atmosphere where that idea can be put into practice and can succeed in bringing a benefit to the organization.

> ### Case study 1: Innovative approaches to service management in the internal market
>
> The market testing programme in UK government departments has led to a number of central functions being contracted out. In some cases, professional functions are now operated as if they were independent businesses within the department. Among the examples are a management consultancy function that previously operated as an inspectorate in a central London department, and the publications operation of an agency that offers a service to other government departments. The financial regime has been organized in these cases to ensure a level playing field when tender bids are being evaluated, for example by ensuring that sums equivalent to value added tax or business rates are included in the costs of the bidders.

Characteristics of the intrapreneur

A survey of UK school principals was carried out in 1993, which identified the desirable characteristics of educational entrepreneurs. It should already be clear that one of the abilities of the intrapreneur is to read across from the possibilities of one situation to another, so let us consider the applications of these characteristics to the library and information professional:

➤vision
➤ability to think long term.

Intrapreneurs need to see the 'big picture', and they need to see the possibilities of a situation. Library and information professionals have a broad canvas on which to paint their vision. Herbert S. White's analysis of the library's position in an organization is probably true in many cases, so that many readers have the potential for development with minimal interference from the rest of the organization. The ability to think long term clearly forms part of that vision. The intrapreneur must consider what influences will affect services in the future, and how services will be continued during the transition and development periods.

This illustrates the importance of a number of management skills that were also identified as important in the survey, such as

➤ the ability to allocate resources for service quality.

This is particularly relevant to the management of service development and innovation.

Then come more standard management skills:

➤ ability to delegate
➤ ability to organize.

Interestingly, the remaining characteristics relate to team working and management:

➤ ability to reduce individual and team stress
➤ acceptance of responsibility of leadership
➤ ability to motivate at all levels
➤ ability to select a good team
➤ ability to develop a good team.

We shall be looking in more detail at team management issues in Chapter 6.

A further survey published by the think-tank Demos identified five requirements to allow the growth of intrapreneurship (in the guise of civil entrepreneurship):

➤ encouragement of risk-taking
➤ financing, rewarding and recognizing innovation
➤ improved means for dissemination of innovation in the public sector, for example through the adoption of 'lessons learned' units (see Case study 2). This idea is already widely used in the USA: many military establishments and some government agencies routinely post information about their lessons learned on their websites

➤ providing political leadership – for example through the local government reforms likely to follow the first directly elected mayors such as that proposed for London

➤ development of a new breed of public sector managers who are trained and motivated as intrapreneurs.

Case study 2

There are as yet few 'lessons learned' published for libraries. But in Boston, Massachusetts, the Research Library for RCRA (the Resource Conservation and Recovery Act) uses this technique to disseminate information – and to plead for resources. Its web presence is a mix of marketing, political lobbying, and demonstration of skills. Thus the head of the library, with only 1.5 full time equivalent staff, is able to point to the unique resources in his library, and to the fact that they are used not only locally but by three foreign national governments as their primary resource. He also raises political issues about the status of the library staff who are contractors rather than federal government staff, and the need to define their terms of reference. Perhaps most intriguing is that some expanding (for which read intrapreneurial) functions of the library, charged with creating local research collections across New England, have been hindered by the lack of transport. The library reports that as an interim measure one of the contractors is using a private vehicle and collecting mileage payments in order to service these collections, but the cost is proving a restricting factor in library development.

The benefits of a proactive style are, as we see in the next chapter, essential for the continuing preservation of the information and library service. There will also be benefits in ensuring that the service continues to provide essential professional input to communities and organizations long after the end of the current fad for generalist managers to embrace information and knowledge management.

In this chapter we have seen that:

➤ new, intrapreneurial roles are opening up for information and library professionals in all walks of the profession

➤ it is important that the information intrapreneur has a particular approach to the users and customers of the service, regardless of where he or she works, and adopts a behaviour style that may be thought somewhat brash for the image of the profession!

Chapter 2
The organization and the information intrapreneur

Intrapreneurs work within an employing organization to achieve their aims but in doing so they must further the ends of that organization. They have to understand not only their own position and activities, but also how these relate to the employer's business. The opportunities for intrapreneurial behaviour thus become clearer.

> **In this chapter we shall look at:**
>
> ➤ **ways to find out what the organization's objectives are**
> ➤ **who the 'movers and shakers' are**
> ➤ **how people use information**
> ➤ **how the intrapreneur fits into these patterns**
> ➤ **how the intrapreneur squares up to knowledge management.**

What is the 'organization'?

An organization in our context can be any body that employs librarians or information specialists (in the sense both of engaging them to work there and of calling upon their services). Members of that organization can be few or many, selected or open to all. Examples could range from a small company or society to the public at large, being served through large public or private organizations or universities and other educational bodies. And it is irrelevant whether the librarian is paid or voluntary; well-considered intrapreneurial behaviour might contribute greatly to a charity's efforts.

Finding out about the organization

The information specialist working within the organization will have a number of routes to find out about the aims and objectives of the body, some formal and some informal. They may be people-based or document-based. They include:

➤ organizational publications
➤ people within the organization
➤ library-derived information
➤ library-sponsored research.

Organizational publications

Most if not all of these organizations, or the library that serves them, will put out a variety of reports which will make it possible to identify opportunities for intrapreneuring. Company information in the UK should be easily available because of the obligation to make an annual return to Companies House. A company is also likely to produce a report for shareholders and others and these documents will contain information about the activities of the company and provide clues to areas in which information services could be developed. Other bodies produce similarly useful documents. Charities and government departments, for example, produce annual reports similar in style to company reports, whilst local authorities have also moved in this direction to provide charge-payers with information about council activities. Universities produce extensive information, including an annual prospectus. Aims and objectives may well be listed in these publications, and if not, they can be deduced from the narrative. Whilst these reports inevitably look back, they will also provide some clues about current and future concerns.

Newsletters of various kinds are a source that amply repays the time spent reading them. You may be certain that any initiatives or projects that are mentioned in them will be close to the hearts of those concerned, and may well be their pet projects. Contacting people and offering support and development ideas will be made easier using such publications, which are often left in information points and libraries by their producers. Best of all, the key people will probably be named in the article, and their telephone numbers or e-mail addresses included too.

People within the organization

It would be an advantage, of course, if the librarian of an organization did not have to resort to reading public documents to find out what was happening or likely to happen. It should be possible to keep in touch with developments through the organization's communications channels – and simply by talking to other people there. (Nothing replaces walking around and discussing information needs and resources with potential and actual clients.) The library and information staff should be talking to:

➤ established users
➤ potential users
➤ rising stars.

Established users

It is surprisingly simple to overlook established users as a source of information about the organization. Yet many of them will be willing to tell you what is going on in their area (whether that is a department of an office, a faculty of a university, or a neighbourhood of a town) and allow the library and information staff to identify resources to support these developments. The librarian possessing natural sociability will help to establish good relationships and networks that can assist the users.

Potential users

Just as important are potential users – those who have not yet realized that information can make a difference. Studies in Canada and the UK have demonstrated that information resources, once potential users have been alerted to them, have an important input to business processes. The library and information professional needs to read the clues to produce a service to suit the potential users (if necessary by asking them about their information requirements).

Rising stars

In the light of the previous two categories, the rising stars – people destined to be prominent in the organization in the near future – are perhaps the most interesting and important group of users to identify. The difference between them and the other groups is that they will develop new areas of work or society, whereas the current and potential users from the core area represent present requirements and demands. Information can be an important tool in the career of the rising star, and the library and information professional can usefully be identified with that career. In the local authority context, for example, gaining a local personality as a user will be a selling point for the service. In a company a new director can be enlisted. University users are already used to coming to the library, but association with a new and dynamic area of work will – if suitably acknowledged – give the library greater knowledge of the developing areas of work.

In other words, knowledge of the developing aims and objectives of the organization (as opposed to knowing what was important last year) comes from active involvement by the information and library service in its community.

Champions

Many of these people are capable of acting as champions for information and library services. Unless you are in a very privileged position, it is unlikely that the information and library service manager will be directly represented on the board of directors or other management body of the organization or community. Yet those rising stars whose information use we discussed above, or indeed established directors who are convinced users of information services, can be champions for the information and library services.

Some doubt has been expressed about the life expectancy of each new incarnation of the basic principle of information and library work – currently 'information management' and 'knowledge management' – and those associated with the start-up phase of these initiatives are often considered vulnerable as the trends go out of fashion. Five years is reckoned to be a good average, with information management at the end of its cycle and knowledge management likely to be renamed in some way by 2000.

Yet the style of behaviour that we are concerned with here is adaptable. It does not matter what words are used to describe the style of activity or its contribution to the organization. What matters is the managerial, businesslike approach to information services, and the frame of mind that goes with managing it.

Library-derived information

A library is a place that should be guaranteed to be packed with relevant information. Yet many library and information professionals are so busy processing information that they fail to use it fully themselves. We are talking less about books and journals on professional topics, but rather more about the press summaries, current awareness bulletins, and other information products that you produce. Be your own most critical customer. Using your own products to gather information about what the organization or community is doing will not only inform you, it will show up information gaps whilst allowing you to share the customers' level of awareness.

Library-sponsored research

Taking this principle further, use your collection to research issues concerning the organization or community. Even if the collection itself does not yield all the answers, a combination of abstracting services and online and Internet searches ought to provide sufficient references to identify key topics and assess the reliability of the available information. Try compiling dossiers of information as a library training exercise, and distribute copies of the most useful ones (remembering to observe any copyright or licensing restrictions that may apply). Discover how often they need to be updated to retain a cutting edge. Read your own abstracting or current awareness bulletins from the customer's viewpoint. If you apply a kind of gap analysis of what you know about the organization and what you would like to know to sell your service most effectively, you will be able to identify ways to improve the bulletin. And the process of finding out and assessing the bulletin will provide you with additional valuable information about the parts of the organization you need to reach.

More about organizational publications

Earlier we looked at literature produced by an organization for public consumption. These could be reports required by statute or sales information (which includes prospectuses) but they could in other contexts be local newspapers or information sheets. Newspapers produced on a small scale for communities, societies or companies tend to rely heavily on local personalities; in a company, for example, a house newspaper will try to include comments and photographs of staff members to help personalize a story. These stories can be helpful; so too can be inviting the newspaper for a photo opportunity with one of these personalities in the library.

Variety is important. Repeated reporting of the same service gives the impression that the information and library service has but a single string to its bow. Readers should constantly be surprised by the variety and usefulness – and quality – of the services they are offered.

Word of mouth

But all the newspaper coverage on earth will not help if there is no dialogue with you and about you. Above, we recommended pounding the beat and meeting customers, actual or potential. Yet useful word-of-mouth promotion of the library need not involve the library staff. Recommendations are of particular value, and can be generated by delivering excellent service to the leading local personalities. Anecdotal evidence suggests that libraries benefit from considerable goodwill, and that even quite mediocre service tends to be praised. How much praise is a truly excellent service likely to generate?

What sort of information is used – and what is it used for?

Every collection should be tailored for its users, so that maximum use is made of it. Every book its reader, and every reader his book – the trick is to bring the readers and the books together in the right place at the right time. So it follows that library and information professionals should be seeking to know what sort of information is used by their clients, and how they use it, in order to ensure that the collection best meets their needs. This clearly applies to any kind of library collection, although it is rather easier to develop the techniques in closed organizations such as companies. However, even in a community library there will be some obvious categories of publications that are unsuitable, whilst the age profile of the library patrons or the geographic location of the library may indicate the need for a strong collection in some other subject. In other areas perhaps there is a preponderance of small businesses that do not support a library of their own and need information and reference support.

The studies in Canada and the UK referred to in Chapter 1, together with earlier work on the use of libraries carried out by Margaret Slater, show both the importance of information and of libraries, and the underuse that is made of them.

How the information professional squares up to knowledge management

Knowledge management is a relatively new technique, which is attracting increasing attention, particularly in mainstream management and IT literature. Typical terms to describe it include:

➤ disclosure or sharing of knowledge (e.g. lessons learned, best practices) so that members of an organization can use that knowledge in their roles within the organization
➤ ensuring that information is available at the location where it is most crucial for decision-making processes
➤ ensuring that knowledge is available when it is needed
➤ ensuring that it is possible for new knowledge to be created, e.g. through research and development operations
➤ ensuring that everyone in the organization knows who has knowledge and where it is.

Information and library professionals will recognize these terms. A library or document centre helps to share knowledge, especially when professional skills are applied to its organization. The second and third points amount to 'the right information (or book, or document) at the right time in the right place' and come remarkably close to the principles set out by Ranganathan. The operations of special libraries, and increasingly of others serving specialist sectors of the community at large, support the creation of new information. And library catalogues are a formal means of recording the whereabouts of knowledge and information, supplemented by the librarians' informal networks and 'clearing house' function, putting users in touch with one another to promote shared objectives.

Put another way, the new techniques of knowledge management call for the skills that librarians have had all along. They are certainly about locating information in documents and organizing the retrieval of those documents to respond to requests for knowledge. But they also involve 'knowing what we know', that is, knowing what information resides in an organization and knowing who has it. This is something that librarians have also been doing informally for years. And librarians are good at ensuring relevant information is shared: one of the recurring themes in knowledge management literature is the problem of people who believe knowledge (or information) is power and do not share it with colleagues, thus destroying the possibility of increasing knowledge through synergy.

In fact, a major problem in many organizations is that the adoption of knowledge management entails recognition of the power that goes with the understanding of knowledge flows and ownership within the organization or community. Quite simply, it puts the librarian into a stunningly strong position, perhaps stronger than that of some leading figures (such as directors).

A change of style

It follows that, though their existing skills are important, librarians do need to change their behaviour, as we suggest throughout this book. First, they need to take a wider view of their professional interest within an organization, so that they use their skills to address not only information (particularly printed information) but knowledge, including who knows what, who knows whom, and where the knowledge resides. For this reason, there are great political advantages for those libraries that undertake a range of functions, such as maintaining the organizational directory or managing public contacts by letter or telephone, as well as maintaining the library. Second, librarians need to act as if their role mattered, and be willing to promote both themselves and their achievements at every level.

That view is endorsed by some of the key players in knowledge management. Thomas Davenport, professor of information management at the University of Texas, Austin, and co-author with Larry Prusak of *Working knowledge: how organizations manage what they know*, says in an interview about the book: 'We both have a lot of admiration for librarians and have been heartened by the role they have begun to play in knowledge management. They need to change some things about how they do their work, but the awareness and application of knowledge have always been at the center of their jobs.' And in an article about knowledge management in the operations of pharmaceutical company Glaxo Wellcome, Sandra Ward, the director of their UK information services, notes, 'It's important that companies exploit the skills of people with librarianship and published information backgrounds.' Work on defining the role of the chief knowledge officer (CKO) in organizations has identified a series of tasks for this person, including:

➤ content acquisition and management
➤ information audit – identification of internal information sources
➤ design of content management tools
➤ putting a structure on the information
➤ understanding external sources
➤ enabling timely delivery
➤ design of communication formats
➤ effective utilization of information.

Some of these topics we examine in more detail in this book – notably information audit, which forms the subject of the next chapter. But again there is nothing in the role of the chief knowledge officer that falls outside the competences of the library and information professional. These roles are allied. The only influence that the CKO can perhaps bring to bear more strongly is a political influence, and even here the library professional's fortunes are beginning to change.

The topic of knowledge management is far more detailed than we have room to examine in this book. But one warning and further opportunity seem to be warranted, both arising from disillusionment with the first phase of knowledge management as it has been applied in some organizations.

The warning is that the loss of enthusiasm for knowledge management that can be brought about by the realization of its complexity may lead to the departure of its champions. So it is as well for the information and library professional to stress through sound marketing that knowledge management is only part of his or her range of skills.

The opportunity also arises from this disillusion, when it is realized that nobody can build a knowledge base covering all knowledge. At the moment where the organization decides instead to concentrate on organizing and indexing what it already knows and owns, the library and its catalogue are revealed as the treasure house of the intelligent, learning organization. The intrapreneurial information and library professional will already have prepared for that event.

In this chapter we have looked at a wide range of topics arising from the intrapreneurial approach to library and information work. We have shown that:

➤ there is a wide range of material that can help you learn about the organization or community that you serve

➤ there are ample opportunities to develop services once you have this knowledge

➤ ideas of the moment, such as knowledge management, draw on skills that the library and information professional already possesses, and are only reinventing the wheel

➤ the intrapreneurial library and information professional has not only the skills but the right to play a prominent part in these developments

➤ political skills are required to ensure that the information and library service is not swept away along with knowledge management if it, or any other fad, is supplanted as further trends emerge.

Chapter 3
The internal information audit

In this chapter you will learn:

➤ how to determine and describe the organization's real information needs
➤ how to find out where customers of the information and library service are in the organization
➤ why people in the organization go elsewhere for information
➤ how to identify who really needs information
➤ how to provide the information when it is needed
➤ the importance of producing the information in the format customers need.

In the previous chapter we looked at the aims and objectives of the organization and their relevance to the information professional. We saw that the information professional who has an understanding and appreciation of these issues is far better able to provide a service that appears relevant in the eyes of the senior managers and other influential figures in the organization. Operating a service that appears to be in a vacuum or somehow isolated from the needs of the organization brings the danger of the service being sidelined or even closed, when with a better understanding of the issues the information service could fulfil an essential role.

Information professionals have one of their most difficult jobs in getting a clear understanding of their organization so as to be able to provide an information service that is central to the organization. The other side of this coin is that they also have to get the organization to understand the nature of professional information management, particularly in those sectors such as finance, management, and government, where every member of staff could be said to be an information worker. A key element is for the information professional to do this in a way that emphasizes his or her understanding of the organization rather than appearing to mount a defence of a library under attack, or set up some form of counter-culture.

Organizations generally have a wealth of information that is held by the various departments, divisions, sections and even individual staff members. Before a relevant service can be provided the information professional needs to build up a picture of the organization's information assets, their relations to one another, and the areas in which they are deficient (causing people to go elsewhere or use informal networks).

Information audit

The tool by which this is done is an information audit. We believe that it has equal potential in public service and academic environments as in the special library services where it was first developed. It is an important and valuable technique that yields data about the information resources held within the organization or community, its match to the information requirements of the customer group, and the opportunities for intrapreneurial behaviour.

An information audit will seek to answer a number of questions about information and its use in the organization. It will pose a number of questions that should persuade management (or the people funding the service) of the value of time and effort spent on the information audit activity. And it will consider a number of problems that may be met in the organization's use of information.

The information audit questions

Issues for an information audit:

Consider the following:

➤ what information is essential to support the main activities of the organization?

➤which information sources support the organization's programme of work, products and markets?

➤who uses them?

Are these information sources:

➤essential
➤desirable
➤nice to have
➤needed to verify other sources?

Are they internal or external? Where does the information reside (in which departments, and in how many copies)? Find out:

➤how up to date the information is, and how it is maintained (both in terms of content and to ensure all copies are the same)
➤where the gaps are in current provision and information flows.

Ask individual members of staff 'On what information do you depend to do your job?'

Undecided management

Undecided management may need to be convinced that an information audit is required. If the organization cannot answer all the following questions positively an information audit should be considered. In each case the same issues as they might apply in a public sector or local authority service are given in parentheses.

➤Are you certain that you have effective control of information resources and the organization's expenditure on them? (or, in the public sector, of the budget that funds them).

➤Can you say what the organization's main information needs are and whether they are satisfied? (Or, what are the client group's main information needs and does the service satisfy them?)

➤How many different computer-based information systems exist already and what information do they contain? Is the information reliable and compatible? Would they all provide the same accurate answer to a given question? (What do your major customers already use as information services? Do they provide reliable information? Are you holding different answers to those questions?)

➤ How many staff use external information services already, e.g. online databases, the Internet, CD-ROMs? Are these better than internal sources? (What external information services do you – and your customers – have access to? Do you have, or need, a budget?)

➤ Are all staff members fully trained and able to use the computerized services and technologies? (Same question)

➤ If not, how much training is needed and at what level? (Same question, plus budget issues).

Problems

A number of typical problems need to be addressed alongside the information audit. The following are common discoveries. You may find others that are specific to your situation.

➤ There may be poor information sharing, and information hoarding (because information is power). Clients may not tell you what they already hold or know, so that you waste time and money finding it again.

➤ Sections and individuals may develop uncoordinated and duplicated information sources. The same information may be being paid for twice over. Would or could your clients pool or share information? Could a business or any other kind of information club provide a cost-effective means of coordinating without asking people to divulge commercial secrets?

➤ Out-of-date information may be being used, likewise information that is not authoritative, or that is incomplete. In many cases this is worse than no information at all. Disasters caused by a failure to check basic facts cannot be excused.

➤ Information may be delivered late, or to the wrong place, or at too high a cost. This is also worse than no information at all.

➤ Lack of telecommunications, e.g. no e-mail facilities, can slow up information delivery or restrict the types that can be delivered.

➤ Clients may be using external information sources. Should you offer to send them information by e-mail? Do you want to lose business to the local cybercafé and their resident information guru – or should you explore the possibility of their opening a branch in your building? (If your managers will not countenance such ideas, make them understand the importance of partnerships, and point out that this is already happening in many forward-looking towns and cities.)

➤ Lack of software development may also slow up information delivery or restrict the types that can be delivered. If the organization sets low standards in its systems, should you consider running more modern systems on standalone machines?

➤ Staff may lack training in information skills, so that untrained staff are looking for information, missing some of it, and interpreting other parts poorly.

Defining information resources and services

To define the information service and how it addresses these issues, you must be consistent in the questions asked and in the interpretation of the answers. To do this you need to define at the outset the various terms used to describe information and library service activities. Librarians often fail to realize they have a trade jargon, and there is frequent ambiguity in its meaning (terms such as routing and circulation have multiple meanings and differ between US and British English).

What is described as 'information services' covers a wide range of activities, which may include libraries, information centres, graphics, records, photocopying, printing, public enquiry services, document management, call centres, database services, etc.: all these will need defining.

In the following we raise some issues to be addressed, and which may help to spark off issues relating to your particular situation.

Typical services provided by libraries and information centres include:

➤ acquisition of stock within defined cost limits
➤ loan of stock items
➤ purchase, receipt, and circulation of journals
➤ loans from other information centres
➤ literature searches
➤ quick reference enquiries

➤ document delivery
➤ indexing
➤ cataloguing.

Depending on the exact nature of the service, there may be technical functions connected with databases, information technology support, and network management. There are probably also some financial functions connected with accounting for and charging out publications and online database search costs.

Telecommunications and networks

Ascertain what the organization's computer department has installed already, and what plans there may be for future developments. If the telecommunications service comes under a different manager then repeat the audit questions. You will need to find out exactly what equipment staff members have available to them for use in their daily work. Until you know the answers you may be unaware of the need to deliver information in certain formats.

Typical questions

Typical questions to be elaborated and asked are:

1 What telephone equipment does each staff member have access to (e.g. voice mail, e-mail, fax into own computer, fax nearby, or central fax machine)?
2 Is the network available to all staff? Does everyone know how to use it fully?
3 Is the office automation system standalone on individual computers or is it networked?
4 Is the same word-processing system (and version) available for everyone? Are there conversion and compatibility problems? Can files be transmitted across the network and if so can they include graphics, tables, embedded objects, etc.? Is there a central policy on version control and updates, and on archiving final versions of documents? (In public services: do you need to offer a range of IT plat-

forms, e.g. PC and Macintosh, and do you always need to have the latest software upgrades available?)

5 Do staff keep their own manual records and files or is there a central registry?

Additional questions

There are some additional questions relating to the use of the network by the LIS for information delivery:

6 Is the network available for broadcast delivery of information e.g. global e-mail, out-of-hours access? How long does it take to deliver a message? And does anyone ever act on error messages when delivery fails?

7 Can the network cope with large quantities of data, either multiple messages or graphics files? If so, does this apply at all times of the day?

8 Is it possible to link the network to external services, either directly or through an approved firewall or router?

9 What permissions and technical clearances are required and how long do they take to obtain? Can individual members of staff also obtain these permissions in order to access services from their own desks?

The objective of the audit

The information audit or mapping exercise should give senior management an opportunity to be able to see systematically:

➤ the true cost and value of currently held information
➤ the need for, and cost of, information that should be acquired
➤ the training needs for staff to be able to most effectively use the information
➤ the need for a comprehensive, more holistic type of information system.

Samples of some matrix profiles tried and tested in an engineering environment to map the result of such a survey are given in Appendix 1.

These can be adapted to help you identify the information held, the information gaps, and other problems.

Underlying issues for the information auditor

Some aspects of information audits may be considered routine, and an audit may be carried out by someone without an information professional's training. However, there are a number of underlying professional issues that need to be taken into account by the information auditor. If the information professional is not carrying out the audit or is not a part of the audit team, his or her commentary on the draft report should take into account the following issues.

What are the organization's real information needs?

We looked at these issues in the previous chapter. There is a range of documents that can help all information professionals, but especially those new to an organization, to discover clues to the real needs of the organization. It is worth stressing that many senior and experienced non-information professionals may well have difficulty taking a high-level view of the organization's needs rather than those of their own section: the information professional has to take the overall view that might be shared by senior company management as well as the more detailed views that will illustrate the work of individual sections.

Where are the customers?

In any organization, large or small, there are always people who have a good, and often accurate, idea of what information they need for their jobs. Others will attempt to do your job for you and ask for particular sources that they think may contain relevant information. However, there are many who do not think they are ever in need of information! And some may need to be shown that information is vital for their work and perhaps their long-term career.

Customers can be grouped into the following categories:

➤ non-users, who claim never to use information

➤ sporadic users, who think they have all the information they need but may occasionally use the information service

➤ timid users, who would like to know more about information but often consider their requests are disturbing other essential LIS work

➤ devoted information users, who make good use of all the services on offer.

Marketing and promotion of information services are discussed in more detail in Chapter 8.

Who needs information?

To help you ascertain who needs information and in particular what kind of information they need, we refer again to the matrix profiles in the appendix. You will need to have a copy for each staff member or client group you interview, and you will note that there are a number of types of profiles for experts, non-experts, etc. You can adapt these for your own use.

Spreadsheets can be used to print and store these matrices, and possibly to analyse them. Tables in word-processor files or constructed in HTML can be read using web browser software, but in this case analysis will be manual and more labour intensive. In some environments, advanced statistical analysis tools may be available to carry out the task.

Where do people go for their information if not to the information service?

There are a number of reasons why people do not use their information and library services. Many people may lack information searching skills and are unaware of the wealth of information that can be obtained. Likewise, many people think they know the answers to all their information needs and carry on without checking to see if more up-to-date information exists. Others consider their requests are unimportant and are prepared to risk the accuracy of their work by guessing or using old information instead of consulting the LIS for up-to-date information.

The crucial question for each individual and section is 'On what information do you depend to do your job or run your business?', followed by 'Is it available within your organization or community?'

External sources of information

These questions will reveal that some individuals may choose or even need to use external sources to obtain information without going through the library or information centre. It may be that they are using the information service of their professional body. If your organization pays for their membership it may be possible to make an arrangement whereby you can have access also to this external source. Corporate subscriptions are often placed centrally but publications included in the cost may not reach the LIS and will thus be wasted. Small businesses may rely on trade associations but will be unable to afford comprehensive coverage of current information.

In the special library field, another commonly found external source is the papers and proceedings of conferences and seminars attended by staff members who obtain these documents and other information that may be of further use to the organization. Arrangements could be made to obtain this information for indexing purposes and then allow the individual to keep the documents on extended loan. This way others in the organization can share the new knowledge.

Experts

If the organization hires external experts to carry out work then the information and library service should negotiate to receive copies of any reports they produce for indexing and for future use. A user community may well include experts on particular topics of interest to that community, and these experts should be encouraged to record their knowledge in a similar fashion.

Computer-based information systems and databases

These services deserve particular attention in the audit. Some may be provided by the LIS, some provided by the owners of your organization's network, and some purchased (by the LIS or the system managers) from external sources. There are a number of types of databases, detailed below, and users' requirements should be noted, as well as what they currently receive. In this context it is of particular interest to discover what people receive directly, perhaps indicating that they attach sufficient value to information on the topic to contribute funding of their own.

➤ Bibliographic databases, which contain records of information either held in the organization or in other collections. These can also be of various types:

- indicative, where the record gives the brief details of author, title, publisher etc.
- informative, where the record gives fuller details and perhaps some keywords to describe the document more fully
- extensive, where the record contains details as above but also a detailed abstract that may allow the user to decide whether the full document is needed.

➤ Databanks, which contain numeric information, chemical formulas etc.

➤ Full text databases, which include references and the full document.

➤ Databases of internal reports – either bibliographic records and/or abstracts of reports generated by the organization's staff and for the organization, or possibly full text. (Some of these documents, e.g. council papers, may become public documents at a later stage and may be held in various formats, both in terms of their content and their physical or electronic format.)

➤ Directory databases, containing names, departments, and telephone, fax, e-mail contacts, etc.

➤ Selective current awareness news services (SCANS) (or a similar name), a selective dissemination of information or current awareness service that gives references to newly acquired documents and other information sources. The SCANS could be sent either by print or electronically to information seekers.

Increasingly, organizations are introducing intranets, internal desktop information services that are almost always based on Internet browser technology – although text-based systems are also found. They contain a number of the services listed above and the LIS should have a key role in defining and managing these systems. Library and information professionals have expertise in a number of key areas in intranet development, including an understanding of information structures and thesaural links, and of the operation of retrieval systems and search engines. With the involvement of library and information professionals, the intranet should be a well-structured system whose pages include much useful information – but there are too many constructed by unaided IT sections bearing witness to what can go wrong if the focus is on technology and not on information.

When is the information needed?

It is essential to find out from the information seeker/user/customer how quickly the information is required. You will need to define the timescales so that everyone is working from the same starting point. A list of definitions will help to achieve consistency and also verify in the customer's mind the time the information must be received.

An example typology of information need might be:

➤ desperate – must have the information within the hour if possible (you may have to remind the customer that extra payment is needed for this kind of speedy service, especially if this is set out in your service level agreement. Your suppliers may use different terminology, so check!)
➤ urgent – needed within 24 hours
➤ as soon as possible – within five working days
➤ non-urgent need – would like at some point in the next two weeks.

How does the customer require the information to be presented?

It is essential that the customer is asked at the time of the enquiry how the presentation of the information should be made. It may be required downloaded onto a floppy disk; it may be required by e-mail; it may be required as a summary followed by other data; or it may be required printed out. The references may need to be organized by author or chronologically arranged. In *Success at the enquiry desk*, another title in this series, Tim Owen stresses the importance and the need to present the information in a professional manner. Do check with the informa-

tion seeker that the services are required or you will be wasting your
time – and theirs, plus valuable resources!

> The final results of the analysis of your information audit should give
> you:
>
> ➤ a unique understanding not only of the organization, but of the
>   behaviour of the information seekers in your organization
> ➤ knowledge of who are the customers in your organization
> ➤ an awareness of who uses information to the fullest extent
> ➤ knowledge of who needs information
> ➤ an understanding of the shortcomings of the telecommunications,
>   computer and other services.
>
> Armed with this knowledge you will be able to:
>
> ➤ create information services to satisfy the information needs of the
>   organization
> ➤ promote and market with precision.
>
> In the next chapter we shall see how the results of the information audit
> are one factor which can be used to help design relevant services even
> before the customer recognizes the need.

Chapter 4
Keeping one step ahead of the customers

In this chapter you will find out:

➤ why it is essential that the information staff keep up to date
➤ how to give the answers before the questions are asked
➤ how to communicate the information message
➤ how to market the information service.

Why it is essential that the information staff keep up to date

Keeping one step ahead of the customers is essential if the information and library service is to be a success. Each staff member of an information service must keep up to date in a number of areas, such as:

➤ knowing what is happening in the organization, be it a local authority, a company, a government department, an academic institution, or a commercial organization
➤ knowing what is happening in the information supply industry, especially developments in tools and technology
➤ knowing about the latest publications in the subject areas covered including books, reports, standard specifications (national and international), legislation (e.g. European and UK), journals and newsletters
➤ knowing about the latest electronic publications such as databases, CD-ROMs and Internet based resources
➤ knowing about the various strategies – local, national and perhaps international that may affect your service, e.g. plans announced by your regional library cooperative, the British Library, or IFLA.

We showed in Chapter 2, when speaking of the rapid development of knowledge management, that the librarian's existing networking skills were an essential means of helping to map knowledge and information flows in an organization or community: that going right back to Dr Johnson's dictum, it is as important to know where or with whom knowledge resides as it is to know something ourselves. And we showed in Chapter 3, when we considered the information audit, that knowing the customer's requirements really does help you as the information specialist to provide up-to-date information.

Customers' expectations

We know that most customers have expectations, make demands upon the information services (which sometimes cannot be fulfilled), and have perceptions of what the service may or may not provide. This is a source of potential conflict between the intrapreneurial service and the customer – particularly where you appear to be neglecting or discarding traditional work to focus on new and more exciting services. Discontinuation, in the name of intrapreneurial service development, of a little-used facility that is highly valued by a senior personality is dangerous – unless you have the results of an information audit to hand!

Where users question the need for the intrapreneur's new approach to these old-style services, it may be necessary to point to documents recording their creation and the expectations for them. In Chapter 7 you will see how important a service level agreement can be in helping to define the services that you can reasonably be expected to give and that the customer can reasonably expect to receive.

We also show how the customer has responsibilities. All these activities, including regular feedback, help shape the delivery of excellent information services.

Giving the answers before the questions are asked

So, how can you give answers before the questions are asked by your customers?

During the information audit (see Chapter 3) you will have amassed a great deal of knowledge about your customer base, whatever kind of organization or community you are working in. You should have a reasonable idea of where your customers are located, the type of information they need (or think they need), their current information demands, and most importantly their future plans of work. From this knowledge you will be able to help the customer keep ahead, whether he or she is a lecturer needing to know the latest information in order to keep ahead of the students or a member of the research team in an organization. This can be done in a number of ways, and we give some case studies to show some ideas of how you can keep one step ahead of the customers.

Case study 3

In the commerce and technology department of a public library you have a number of companies that are members of the local information network. They all need to know when the latest pieces of legislation on (for example) the environment have been published. You can check legislation on the Stationery Office Limited site (formerly HMSO) on the Internet, which is updated on a daily basis, and then send an e-mail or fax to the named contact in that company. Information taken from related government websites would provide further information. You might wish to provide this as a value added service and charge accordingly for it.

Case study 4

You are a company information officer and your company's health and safety manager needs to know the latest piece of information from the Health and Safety Executive or Commission (HSE/C). You can either subscribe to the HSE/C Press Release Service or check the HSE webpages, which are regularly updated. You may also subscribe to the Health and Safety Commission Newsletter, which is published six times per year, and check for any retrospective item that you may have missed, or obtain a summary of the latest relevant European legislation. With these sources or a combination of them you can provide a service that is constantly abreast of official developments in the field.

Case study 5

You are the subject specialist of an academic library. The engineering department has asked you to keep it up to date on some specified areas of research. Your course of action is to establish profiles of the requirements on a number of databases and CD-ROMs that are available and then provide a selective dissemination of information (SDI) service. You might also consider drawing upon some of the excellent engineering Internet sites, such as the University of Edinburgh Engineering Virtual Library site, although this will obviously involve you in evaluating the sites both for quality and relevance to your users' interests. You will need to agree with your customers how often they need an update of information; do remember to check at intervals that the subjects you are searching for are still the ones that they are currently interested in being kept up to date on!

These generalized case studies illustrate the principles of keeping ahead of the customer. The subject field in which you are working will have its own databases and subject information sources on which you can draw in ways similar to those we have described. (You will need to be careful not to use information on databases in ways for which either the databases or your organization are not licensed.)

Further ways of keeping ahead

Some further ways you can keep ahead of the customer include:

> providing a selective current awareness newsletter of recent items of stock or journal articles which can be sent to the customers either on the traditional paper format or via e-mail. You can include a response form so that the customer can reply by e-mail and ask for a loan or photocopy. If you have an intranet or a service through the Internet, both the bulletin and the response form can be broadcast and the requests returned to you using forms technology

➤ providing training courses, so that customers can use the various databases that you have created and have networked around the organization

➤ providing induction courses for new members of the organization or department

➤ providing regular information sessions updating staff or customers on the new services

➤ offering basic and advanced Internet training courses

➤ creating databases and CD-ROMs to meet your customers' needs

➤ offering local history knowledge or showing how to trace ancestors

➤ offering a search service that could be part of a membership package

➤ offering special membership packages designed for particular groups, e.g. lawyers, doctors, or small businesses

➤ offering to run other organizations' information services on contract

➤ offering to run Internet websites for businesses or hosting a site and allowing 'advertising space'

➤ if permitted, offering space within the information services' premises for appropriate businesses and services, such as bookshops, stationers, cafes or cybercafés.

Quality management

Beryl Morris, in her book in this Library Association Publishing series *First steps in management*, states that a common approach to developing quality in information and library services has been the adoption of total quality management. She says that information and library services are putting considerable efforts and energy in ascertaining customer needs and developing customer-focused services such as those we suggest above.

If you follow the ideas in Chapter 3, 'The information audit', you will amass considerable knowledge about customers' needs, both actual and perceived, where potential customers or lapsed customers are, the level of services needed, the existing competition, and the customers' criteria for recognizing success. It is the list of critical success factors (see below) recognized by the customer that shows whether a particular service is really meeting their needs and whether you are delivering a satisfactory service.

Communicating the information message

Now we turn to the vexing question of how you can communicate the information message. Too often we find that the information service has really wonderful systems and services but no-one in the organization seems to be aware of them.

Most people still have a perception of the library or information centre only as the place where they can escape to avoid other people or quietly pass the time reading the newspaper. So to be sure that the excellent and useful services that you have created are known and used you must take some drastic steps. You need to get it across that there is much to be gained from using the information service in a positive way, and that message needs to be presented in a similarly positive manner.

Presentation skills

Many people are nervous about making presentations. Presentation skills courses address their fears and will typically aim to teach some or all of the following techniques – how to:

➤ overcome the anxiety and fear of speaking to groups
➤ project self-confidence
➤ give persuasive and powerful presentations using techniques suitable for any size of audience
➤ give effective, impromptu presentations without prior planning or notes
➤ use humour in the right ways in the right places
➤ project credibility in your presentations, even when speaking to expert audiences
➤ identify the skills you already have to help you to develop a natural, comfortable speaking style
➤ regain momentum when you've lost your train of thought
➤ handle difficult questions.

Simple techniques

Some simple techniques can help you to win support and to avoid feeling defensive when discussing unpopular or unpleasant subjects – even when listeners are openly hostile.

The use of quotations, anecdotes, and analogies will inform, educate, and entertain your listeners. Never be caught off guard. Real-life examples of enquiries that information and library services answer can be used to illustrate some point, and many of these are amusing or interesting. You should prepare and keep to hand some practical ideas for impromptu or short-notice presentations, which could be used for example when some important visitor is brought in to see the information and library services.

Particularly when dealing with the more technical professional issues, it is perhaps too easy to become dry, boring, or over-technical. Even a specialist audience may be unforgiving, and an audience of non-specialists will quickly be lost by jargon or overemphasis on technical details. Creative presentations of such material will be appreciated by all kinds of audience, and admired by your peers. If you can carry your audience with you whilst you speak you will quickly realize if your message has been misunderstood and know what corrective measures are needed to get your presentation back on track. If you lose your audience, they will give you no signals showing whether they understand your message. The fact that they go away without question or comment does not necessarily show that they understood and agreed with all you said.

The equipment factor

It pays big dividends to learn how to use microphones, audiovisual equipment, and other presentation equipment – and how to think on your feet when equipment fails! Newer equipment such as computer projectors makes it simple to give presentations of a very high quality using a laptop or other computer. Look for or ask for projectors that can relay instructions from their remote control to the computer as if they were mouse clicks advancing the presentation, which allow you to move freely instead of clinging to the end of a mouse cable while you speak.

Presenting colleagues and taking questions

Develop the skill of introducing other speakers with warmth and professionalism. When you are presenting, these people are your colleagues on stage, whatever your relationship with them outside the occasion, and you owe them professional respect.

You may well be happy to take questions during your presentation. Indeed, by answering a short question as you go along, you can often avoid a long recap that wastes valuable question time at the end. But there will always be someone who wants to interrupt your presentation, if not to heckle, then to seek at length some piece of information that may be of little interest to the rest of your audience. Such interruptions and distractions can throw even the best-prepared speakers off-course, but by learning to deal with them you can give a truly professional edge to presentations.

Poor body-language can also distract your audience. If your posture is giving a quite different message from your text, it lowers your effectiveness and sends your audience away confused. Your most honest colleague is better than your mirror for telling you the truth! And none of us is so good that we cannot improve our presentations.

Learning how to market the information service

Organizations and individuals know that accurate, relevant, and timely information is crucial to remaining viable, competitive and ahead of the game in many fields. So it is vital that the information and library services make sure that organizations and managers know the best way to obtain information when it is needed.

Marketing (see also Chapter 8) has a terminology that is new to many information professionals. It uses terms such as 'market segmentation' which describes ways of dividing your total market, containing all your customers and potential customers. The segments can be further divided into smaller groups that may also share common characteristics. For instance, if you are in an academic library the engineering students may form a segment. In a special information service a segment may be the legal staff.

When you have identified the various segments, you will be able to market the particular information service that suits that particular group. You will be able to learn more about this in Keith Hart's book on marketing in this series (see further reading for Chapter 8).

Critical success factors (CSFs)

You need to establish the critical success factors for each service you offer. What would have to happen or be achieved in order for the service to be judged a success? We referred earlier in this chapter to customers' CSFs, and how they can be used to measure the success of your services in their estimation. You should also establish a list of CSFs for your services from the library and information services' point of view. Evaluating your services' achievements against this second internal list will help you decide if a service is worth continuing or needs changing. Having a constant dialogue with the customers will soon give you the feedback you need and ensure that the various lists of CSFs are kept in line with one another.

How to stay ahead

Remember to constantly ask the following questions about each service:

➤ why is it done, need it be continued, can the need for it be avoided?
➤ how is it done, why this way, can a better way be found?
➤ when is it done, why then, can a better time be found?
➤ where is it done, why there, can a better place be found?
➤ who does it, why is it done by him/her/them, would another person/group be better?

Likewise the users should:

➤ be aware of what the information service can do
➤ identify their information problems
➤ communicate these problems and discuss them with the information staff
➤ give feedback to the information service

➤ keep the information services staff aware of their changing subject interests

➤ involve the information services in projects that have information implications.

To summarize, you should be now aware of the following:

➤ why it is essential that the information staff keep up-to-date
➤ how to give the answers before the questions are asked
➤ how to communicate the information message
➤ how to market the information service
➤ know what are the critical success factors.

Chapter 5
Delivering innovative services

In this chapter we look at means of delivering new and innovative services and the opportunities provided by newly developing areas:

➤ the opportunities from new technology
➤ taking part in lifelong learning
➤ the librarian as guide and coach
➤ practical problems in developing services
➤ new partnerships
➤ turning information into a value added service.

There are many opportunities to develop new services which, whilst they may not fit into the traditional mainstream of library and information work, call upon the skills of the library professional. A range of initiatives that are founded on the creative use of information is now being developed at national level in many countries. Library professionals are presented with a range of publicly-backed projects that will benefit from trained professional input.

New technology

It would be easy to devote this entire book to the ways in which new technology and librarians have come together. It is one of the paradoxes of the profession that a group of people perceived as being so traditional have been such enthusiasts for new technology. It comes as a surprise to many to realize that, two decades ago, the precursors of today's fast Pentium PCs were chunky electric typewriters with acoustic couplers built in, working at only one-hundredth of the transfer rates now standard. But even then libraries were using these to access news and database services, and impressing their customers with this amazing new technology.

The technology that is now developing brings a number of opportunities.

Providing access

1   The library can act as an access centre to allow as many people as possible to use computers and online information services.

According to Bill Gates, the CEO of Microsoft Corporation, writing to the Australian Library and Information Association before Australian Library Week 1998, his involvement with and support of libraries in the United States is 'to ensure that people of all communities have access to the Internet. I see it as a great opportunity to reach out and have the world at their fingertips, to seek out and share information and to learn throughout their lives'.

Other successes

In the United Kingdom, Heritage Secretary, Chris Smith MP, launched National Library Week 1997 by describing public libraries as 'the universities for ordinary people, [providing] access to new communications technology for thousands of people without access] at home'.

There are many examples. A new multimedia library opened in March 1998 at Hendon, in north-west London, providing a total of 40 computers to meet the needs of a wide audience. In July 1996 the government of Flanders, the Dutch-speaking part of Belgium, decided to connect all its public libraries to the Internet, with the overriding objective of providing all citizens with an easily accessible connection to information worldwide. (This ease is in terms both of the cost to the user and the assistance offered by library staff, a point we shall examine further below.)

The library and the skill of its staff can help other parts of an organization to reach its public more effectively. In Edinburgh, proposals have been put forward to extend an existing community information system into a new version, named Capinfo 2000, 'to help meet [the council's] needs in providing information to the public'. The lead is being taken through the central library in taking a range of information written, published, distributed, and managed by various departments of the council, and making it available in a variety of formats, including Internet and text TV, to potential customers.

Imaginative use of the technology

2   **Building on this access, the library can act as intermediary to allow disadvantaged and special groups to gain access to the new technology.**

The United States National Commission on Libraries and Information Science summed up this point succinctly in the preface to a report issued in January 1998:

> The Commission is concerned that public libraries offer advanced telecommunications and information services that benefit local communities. Just as they have offered open access to recorded knowledge since the earliest days of our Nation's history, public libraries have a vital role in assuring that advanced information services are universally available to all segments of the population on an equitable basis.

As an extension of this, the library can use new technology to support its programmes. Imaginative use of technology can improve access for some groups of people.

Speakers of minority languages can be better served by access to information in their language even when staff who speak it are absent. Queens Library in New York has 'Las Paginas en Español', which allow the 20% of its population whose first language is Spanish to search the library's catalogue in that language. It also runs programmes to develop Russian and Turkish collections in areas with high immigrant populations. And it provides a multilingual interface to the Internet, WorldLinQ, developed at the library, which allows Chinese, Korean, and other non-roman characters to be displayed on a computer screen. Daily newspapers from China, Taiwan and Korea can be read on the Internet and Chinese libraries accessed from Queens.

In the Western Isles of Scotland, the Gateway Project, successfully submitted to the Scottish Office Public Libraries Challenge Fund by

Comhairle nan Eilean Siar (formerly the Western Isles Council), seeks to generate interest and support for the Gaelic language, and to foster community identity with reference to culture and oral tradition. Coventry Libraries are planning a CD-ROM as a project with the local Irish community which will include the experiences of the community in the UK, its culture, literature, and language.

But it is not only members of minority-language-speaking groups who can benefit from libraries' imaginative use of technology. Rural communities can be disadvantaged by their location, at least so far as access to libraries is concerned. Australia provides many examples. In the Northern Territory, community libraries are typically surrounded by cattle stations or wetlands, yet through links with educational facilities they offer technology-based modern services according to seasonal demand, which varies with the timing of the rains and school terms. In another part of the Territory, the Yulara community library at Uluru (formerly Ayer's Rock) combines resources such as storytelling relating to the Aboriginal people's sacred site with Internet access. In Queensland, public libraries are described as 'the people's on-ramps to the Information Superhighway' despite the 'vast spaces and tyrannical distances' of that state.

In Europe the BIBDEL project (funded under the second call of the European Commission's DG XIII Programme for Libraries) has considered ways of delivering services to remote users, including access and privileges for those remote users. Another DG XIII funded project has looked at the use of new technology on board mobile libraries to support the delivery of library services in rural areas in Greece and the United Kingdom. The Bibliothèque Nationale de France proposes to offer readers remote access to a database of 13 million records (*Le catalogue collectif de France*) through other libraries and documentation centres in France.

Other groups to benefit

Other groups who benefit from innovative use of new technology by libraries include senior citizens. Baltimore County Public Library Senior Center provides an Internet page containing links to resources for senior citizens. Librarians gather information from a range of sources, including directories and flyers, and enter it on a database reached by hyperlinks from the page. And the electronic information is increasingly accessible to the partially sighted, either by enlarging the font size viewed on the screen, or by using software that reads aloud text pasted to the Windows clipboard. Senior citizens may well be able to make valuable contributions in return to local history collections.

Although children are frequently thought of as more technically literate than the rest of the population, they still have some special needs in library services. Queens Library in New York runs a special programme for teenage parents, together with their babies and their own parents, to demonstrate the use of library services for support in parenting and for continuing their education. Children's computer literacy can help to deliver their needs, and UKOLN's Treasure Island Internet pages contain one approach to this.

Enhancing access

3   **The library can use the new technology as a means of processing its collections and as a means of publishing in novel forms, and use the new technology to enhance access to its collections.**

The price of CD-ROM publishing is now lower than conventional print on paper for many applications. For a project such as the Coventry Libraries CD-ROM described above, its cost is enhanced by its capacity to store a range of formats including sound and images. Another of the Scottish Office Public Library Challenge projects is The Virtual Mitchell: this includes plans to digitize materials from the riches of Glasgow's Mitchell Library and its City Archives, and to make these searchable and available over the city council's network and on the Internet.

Lifelong learning and library services

Lifelong learning has been around for far longer than the name that is now applied to it, and libraries have been part of that process for a hundred years or more. Their role in lifelong education provides scope for further innovative services. The UK government's Green Paper *The learning age*, notes that 'the public library service holds an enormous range of educational material and has the potential to deliver information and learning to people of all ages and backgrounds, right across the country. The Learning Age 'will be supported by the development of new information and communication technology within libraries.' Proposals are to be produced for a public libraries IT network as an integral part of the National Grid for Learning.

But this role is not only for public libraries. Others following the principles of Investors in People should consider the role of their library or information centres as open learning centres to support training and development. The use of multimedia technology fits well with the modern corporate or indeed academic library, but the traditional printed book and periodical continue to have a strong claim to a place in this environment.

The librarian as guide and coach

The rapid growth of technology leaves many people in need of help, support, or explanation. Many people in the UK have taken advantage of the series of schemes promoted by the BBC that make use of public libraries to introduce new technology to ordinary users. Under the title 'Computers Don't Bite', new users of computers have been given a 'test drive'.

More generally, library staff are in an ideal position to act as guide and coach to those unfamiliar with new technology. Librarians have long been users of technology. Now the early computerized catalogues of the late 1960s have given way to widespread use of PC networks and the Internet. The librarian's (largely unappreciated) technical knowledge is at last being matched by some reported development of library skills among IT staff.

This traditional role of the library may well be an appropriate one to develop in an intrapreneurial role. In the corporate or academic environment, the library provides a central outlet for mentoring and support services, which aligns perfectly with its role as the central information resource.

Computer-assisted learning

Computer-assisted learning and other services are starting to appear in the more progressive public libraries. In a number of government agencies, the development of open learning facilities has been followed by close working between the library and training sections in recognition of the overlap of interest. In both public and private sector organizations, the installation of extensive IT networks has been accompanied by minimal training: there are constant reports of the banal level of many enquiries to support staff (how do I print the page? how do I get the sticky label out of the printer roller so it works properly again?).

There are, of course, issues of training and development for information and library professionals and support staff. Their initial training provides many of the skills needed to deal with the coaching role; but time and resources need to be devoted to learning familiarity with new software and other facilities. If new services are to be offered, the library service must be confident in its ability to provide, and its users must be confident in the librarians' skills.

Practical problems in developing services

The *New library: the people's network* report points at a number of related issues which, again, are not solely questions for the public library service. For example, longer opening hours are necessary if services are to be provided at times to suit potential users. University libraries have experimented with 24-hour opening, allowing students approaching finals to make use of the (often unattended) service at any time of day. UK public libraries experimented recently with all-night opening during 1997 National Library Week. Special libraries in locations such as hospitals provide access at all hours, though professional service at unusual hours is the exception (media libraries, for instance) rather than the rule – or even the hint of a rule. Yet with more part-time working, home working, and individuals increasingly holding more than one part-time job, the question of library opening hours is clearly important, and finding innovative ways of extending services within existing budgets is a priority.

Even the titles used by library departments indicate the range of services that can be expected nowadays. Certainly, in some local authorities, libraries remain grouped with sports and leisure facilities; but in others a range of cultural and educational activities are grouped. For example, in Essex, a new Learning Directorate includes a Head of Libraries, Information, Heritage and Cultural Services.

Core skills

A survey early in 1997 monitored job advertisements for non-library/information manager posts which nonetheless had information elements within the job description. Research identified core skills as presentation and communication, systems and IT, sector knowledge, creativity and innovation, research analysis, team working, and training skills. In reporting this, Angela Abell remarked that these skills coincide with the attributes of the successful library manager.

In the business setting, the role of the library and information professional must embrace change in many areas of work, and become involved in areas of work far removed from the traditional tasks. In the technical sphere, it encompasses questions such as Year 2000 compatiblity – the so-called Millenium Bug, which may prove to be a bug long past 1 January 2000 – or the use of information in corporate change. Similarly, education is no longer simply a matter of schooling, even though schools library services are a fairly recent innovation in many areas. The development of lifelong learning and support for civic education are two examples of new and information-hungry forms of education far removed from the traditional school curriculum which demand a contribution from the information profession.

New partnerships

Partnerships between publicly funded libraries and the private sector, whilst largely taboo even 20 years ago, are now acceptable and offer opportunities for appropriate development of new services. There was at one time caution about using any materials with commercial connections; in the current climate sponsorship is proving a valuable way of developing new services. The involvement of the BBC with the 'Computers Don't Bite' campaign was mentioned earlier. Of the introductory sessions in the first tranche of this promotion (May 1997), 20% were reported to have come through libraries, and the new wave of activity linked to National Library Week 1997 ran through libraries alone. Newspapers and even toilet-tissue manufacturers make materials available for particular library sectors. In another form of sponsorship, the longer opening hours and Sunday opening considered earlier in this chapter as an innovative service are being provided in some places by local sponsorship. And during 1998 the Literature Department of the Arts Council of England together with The Library Association is examining new areas for potential collaboration with the key players in literature and publishing.

Turning information into a value added service

Information is a commodity whose value is finally being understood and appreciated. Manufacturers and vendors of intelligent agent software promote their products on the basis that the discovery, storage, management and retrieval of information form a complex process whose value warrants their investment. Libraries have of course employed intelligent agents for many years: they are called librarians. The information profession across all sectors adds value to information and interprets or retrieves it for the benefit of its customers.

> To summarize. In this chapter we have seen:
>
> ➤ many examples of approaches to the development of innovative services; interestingly, although we could have quoted extensively from examples taken from special libraries, almost all our examples are from the public and academic library sectors
>
> ➤ a common approach to information, which adds value to it, either by its being appropriate for its particular audience, or by bringing together items that are otherwise separate
>
> ➤ how to build on the traditional strengths of the library service to provide modern services
>
> ➤ how none of the above would happen without the intrapreneurial information professional, whatever library sector we are considering
>
> ➤ why services need to develop; otherwise they stagnate and eventually they are replaced by services of other, new entrepreneurs
>
> ➤ why the intrapreneurial professional looks for the opportunities to develop new value from existing resources, or new resources to develop further value.

Chapter 6
Building the perfect team

In this chapter we consider ways to build the perfect team to put into practice the ideas we discuss in this book. You will find suggestions about:

➤ the ideal skills and knowledge of members of an intrapreneurial library team
➤ training the intrapreneurial library team
➤ risk taking
➤ creating opportunities.

Why the team is so important

Even intrapreneurs take some time away from the workplace. It is a good idea for everyone to recharge his or her batteries and take leave; and nobody is so indispensable that he or she must be at the workplace all day, every day. Even if the intrapreneur is full of energy and never calls in sick, and even if he or she is running a one-man-show, there needs to be some kind of team that can provide backup. Holidays are not a luxury, and what about time to network within the organization or at the occasional conference or exhibition? In the larger organization, the team is doubly important. The business of the library must continue whilst the team leader is away, and so developing a strong team is vital in order to provide a continuing service in line with the leader's intrapreneurial vision.

Much is heard these days of ideas such as 'delayering' and the 'leaner, flatter' organization which became well known through Peters and Waterman in the 1980s. Organizations have been contracting – in both senses of the word. On the one hand, they call on external suppliers to make contracts to supply some services that were previously provided internally. (We discuss this in further detail in Chapter 7.). On the other hand, organizations have been shrinking. Public sector organizations have reduced in size. Private companies have had to trim in order to survive. Mergers are commonplace and so are the mergers of information functions that go along with them. New teams are formed, although some members of existing teams are lost, leading to new development needs to address the new organization goals and team dynamics.

There are certainly advantages to team working, apart from the simple issues of continuity of presence and cover. Complex work plans are carried out better by teams: they can cover a wider range of roles than the individual, they provide quality assurance, and they can ensure that goals are reached even when other important issues intervene. Team members feed off each other's ideas and develop typically more complex and successful solutions to problems than do individuals working alone. And teams can send stronger signals of commitment and involvement in the solution of organizational problems than individuals can do alone.

Skills and knowledge

In this book, we describe skills that belong as much in the boardroom or the council chamber as in the library. So in what follows, it would be as well to assume a high level of professional skill as a foregone requirement. After all, no matter how astute the management skills and however artful the political skills of the intrapreneur, unless he or she can deliver the goods when results are needed against deadlines, there will not be a second chance to use them.

One intrapreneurial librarian can make a difference. A team of like-minded people can be formidable. In a small organization where the library selects its own staff, it should be possible to form a team that will follow a like-minded entrepreneurial path by invitation and selection. This is, sadly, not always the case in larger organizations and the public sector in particular; but at least it is becoming more widely known that the library is not a good dumping spot for inefficient clerical staff who like reading.

Gifford Pinchot offers ten commandments for the intrapreneur, which gives us a starting point in considering the skills that team members require. We are looking as much for a state of mind as for definable skills, and for an attitude to the task in hand as much as for detailed technical knowledge. Perhaps fortunately for the intrapreneurial librarian, the position of the library within many organizations saves the need to go out on a limb from the outset. Despite Pinchot's exhortation to come to work each day prepared to be fired, most librarians are probably safe from this fate, given the kind of activity they tend to undertake and the organization's view of the risk it poses. On the other hand, the organizational structure that tends to surround libraries can prevent some of the more freewheeling approaches, such as forming teams of volunteers to work on risky projects.

These 'high-risk' elements aside, Pinchot's commandments suggest some useful characteristics for team members, and some new ways of working. Team members should be willing to turn their hand to any task needed to bring success to a library project. It is no good trying to run a dynamic, go-getting service with people whose go-getting dynamism stops dead when their support staff are on leave, or see some work as beneath or beyond them. Work with the best, and the best people are flexible.

Job descriptions are useful for saying what people should do, but less so for defining what they should not do. Short of undertaking things that could provoke a strike, the members of an intrapreneurial library should be prepared to turn their hands to the whole range of tasks. If everyone else is busy, and the job has a deadline, then only one person is available do the job: it's that simple, and that person is you. (Of course, one of the skills of management is to make sure that the one person available is also the best person for the job. But if the team is made up of skilled people who are all leaders by nature, that should not be difficult). Pinchot notes the principle that it is easier to ask for forgiveness than for permission. Library team members should think of getting the job done, using the best person available to deliver the best quality job to the customer on time. If long-standing organizational rules (or hierarchies, or traditions) have to be bent to achieve this, then they should be to the extent that this allows the job to be done to the customer's satisfaction.

The rules may prove more flexible than you thought, in which case they will not be broken. And if people really think it a useful way to spend their valuable time, there will be opportunities to argue about it after the deadline, but you should be able to count on the backing of your grateful customer! (This idea should perhaps be taken to extremes only by those who are truly prepared to be sacked each day they arrive for work!)

Hard work is called for. One of the problems of developing innovative services is that the main service needs to be kept going while the development takes place, so you will be looking for flexibility and versatility in team members as a minimum. They will need to be good with people. They will need to convince others – often the movers and shakers – of the value of information, and to do so in a persuasive way rather than a confrontational way. It is not a wise move to suggest that it was about time people realized that the library had the answers all along – even if it did. The movers and shakers of the organization, of the community, of whatever client group the library serves, those people can provide the library with enormous support if they are well served and publicly acknowledge the value of the library service.

Managing the intrapreneurial team

Hierarchical organizations may have trouble managing intrapreneurial teams, which tend to work in a lateral kind of way. This can upset places where instructions and responses are seen to travel up and down a chain of command, and intrapreneurs prefer to work in a way that cuts across hierarchies and structures in order to pull together teams of the people best suited to the task in hand. Organizations are, however, having to change. Many sections of a large organization now have an interest in major projects, and success of a project often depends on the skills and knowledge of a number of people. The information technology function is often seen as critical; so too is the information management function that complements it, and which the intrapreneurial librarian has first claim to manage. And how surprising if that librarian turns out to have been the first to adopt the new ways of working!

Organizations will generally demand that someone be recognized as in charge and responsible for the library or information unit. But skilful analysis of the role of the unit will allow delegation to those best able to lead work on particular issues and functions, so that they can lead task forces on those topics. A number of skills may need to be developed in these team leaders: handling interpersonal relationships, leadership, and communication skills are examples. Team members need to be able to fulfil a number of roles in the teams, sometimes as leaders, sometimes in other capacities. If formal project management techniques are used, team members will need to fill the stipulated roles in those techniques. In other cases, they may need to speak for the library alongside technical or user representatives. They need to have the confidence not only of the library management but the organizational management in doing so, and it is important that necessary training should be provided either through courses or through coaching by taking part, under guidance and supervision, in existing projects.

This rather informal, freewheeling style of working is not without risks. If conflict arises in the team, especially a small one, it can be a difficult way to work. If possible, an agreed means of resolving conflict needs to be built into the team's culture. Perhaps some form of mediation through the head of unit may be adopted, or a team meeting in which an open exchange of views takes place. But it is as well to be aware of the rather delicate balance that exists at the core of the intrapreneurial team; it needs to include people capable of acting decisively and imaginatively on behalf of the team, but it cannot afford prima donnas. The team members should sign up, literally or figuratively, to the intrapreneurial culture, and thus agree on the limits of their own unfettered action, and the means of resolving conflict with other team members or leaders.

Team-playing beyond the information and library service

Knowledge management is widely recognized as a team enterprise. In addition to the intrapreneurial information service teams described above, there is value in forming peer knowledge networking teams across an organization or community – that is, teams that are formed at high level to combine skills and specialist knowledge of different areas, and which may operate on a basis closely resembling continuous brain-storming.

Other specialists, managers, and professionals will balance the information and library service manager's less developed areas of knowledge, and his or her specialisms will in turn balance other managers' shallower knowledge in the field of information management.

All members of an information and library service should be given the opportunity to take part in such community-wide committees and boards. Not only is it good development experience, but differing interpretations of the same events in the wider world should broaden the management team's view of the service.

A particular area of convergence

One type of team operation is worth particular mention. Libraries and IT sections have gone through a period of convergence in recent years that has been well documented: the process need not detain us further here. However, for both sides this combination of library and IT professionals is not without difficulties, which need to be taken into consideration in developing a team working style. Users demand coordinated services, and are uninterested in which part is supplied by a library professional and which by an IT specialist. Many modern library services rely on IT to the point where it is unclear which is the information content and which is the communication technology. Much of what modern librarians do could not be done without information technology.

Yet many of the enquiries put to library professionals make no use of their information management skills but are concerned rather with issues such as making printers work or dealing with slow communication from a remote database or the Internet. It makes good sense in many libraries to manage library IT and library user services within a single team. Yet it is a considerable management problem. On the one hand, the library service must be run competently and professionally, so IT staff without formal library training must be given basic knowledge to allow them to handle simple library enquiries correctly and fully. The other requirement is that library staff have sufficient IT knowledge to deal with some simple and maybe some more complex problems, whilst not feeling that their professional library qualifications are being squandered. Since the staff numbers involved are often quite small, for example when academic libraries cover late evening working with mixed profession teams of this kind, solutions are essential. They are based on a broader consideration of the principles underlying successful team management that could easily apply to intrapreneurial management generally.

In this chapter we have examined some of the issues concerning team working in the intrapreneurial information and library service. We have found that two kinds of team are required:

➤ a team of matched individuals working within the information and library service, who between them can provide the skills and experience to match the customers' needs, and go on to provide innovative, intrapreneurial service

➤ a team outside the information and library service in which the head (or other members) of the service take part, and which drives forward concepts such as knowledge management. This provides the information and library service with channels outward for its views and contributions, and channels inward for information about events affecting the community it serves and the people who are its customers.

Chapter 7
Setting and maintaining standards

In this chapter you will find out:

➤ why standards are needed
➤ how service level agreements help
➤ why performance measurements are essential
➤ how to obtain and act on user feedback.

Why standards are needed

Organizations and individuals know that accurate, relevant and timely information is crucial to remaining viable, competitive, and ahead of the game. So it is vital that information services make sure that organizations and managers know the best way to obtain information when it is needed.

Managers are also very much aware that within an organization is a largely untapped base of information that is not organized in an easily retrievable way. When this information is required it is usually in a hurry. To improve the situation, it is necessary that this information is properly organized. The information and library service is the best situated in any organization to do this, so it should be both central to an organization, be it a university, a commercial organization, a manufacturing enterprise, an association, government body or an agency, and also aware of customers' needs, so as to be able to offer the services required.

If the staff in an organization are unaware of the significance of information and the need for a central information and library service, then it is likely that the decision-making will be flawed. There is also the added problem that duplication of effort may occur, which again creates extra costs. There is a further risk of inefficiency because few staff members have any training in information retrieval skills and techniques, and they are unlikely to be aware of the sources of information that exist outside the organization. Databases, statistics, and other specialist sources of strategic importance may be ignored.

Quite often information resources have been fragmented in an organization because of the need to have costs departmentalized. This can happen when an organization grows fast, merges, or diversifies. The use of personal computers has also contributed to this fragmentation, as people keep their information closely guarded or receive information by way of their job but fail to share it with colleagues or the organization itself. Many people still imagine that information is power; in fact the power is released only in sharing the information, and releasing that power too late can severely damage an organization or community.

The continual development of new technologies such as information 'push' may help management to be able to invest in the organization of all the scattered resources within the organization. There are many helpful published accounts, such as those describing the introduction of knowledge management systems in any of the 'big six' management consultancies or major accountancy firms. Such developments bring many opportunities for the information intrapreneur, who can directly organize these fragmented sources into a cohesive whole; provide corporate tools such as a thesaurus to allow improved access and navigation through information and documents; act as a trainer and navigator for staff; and adapt information and library services so that when there is a demand for information it can be quickly located and synthesized to meet the customer's requirement.

By the use of generally accepted standards, the professionalism of the information and library service is assured in the customer's eyes. By measurement against those standards, the service can certify that it is maintaining professional quality and can reassure the users that there is no need to go elsewhere. And as we show below, by the use of service level agreements, both customer and supplier can agree on those levels and what to do if they are not achieved.

How service level agreements help

A service level agreement is a kind of internal contract that records the agreement between two or more parties about the levels of services being provided (such as information and library services) to their customers. They are very useful in situations where money does not change hands or where the parties all work for the same organization.

The basic objectives of a service level agreement (SLA) are to:

➤ state what the customer needs by providing a service statement
➤ show the mechanics and processes of fulfilling those needs
➤ describe the volumes of activities to be handled and
➤ prescribe the ways of measuring them.

In doing this, the SLA records what the 'purchaser' (the receiver or consumer of the service) wishes to buy (using real money, or a transfer of internal funds on paper) and therefore what the 'supplier' (typically the information and library service) is expected to provide. It sets out the agreed services in such a way that it is precise enough to act as an agreement but not so prescriptive that it prevents service development or precludes negotiated change to improve the service.

It is essential that all levels of staff are involved in the compilation of the SLA, because everyone's personal performance, understanding of the standard and levels of services to be achieved, and the timescales within which these levels of services are to be given are implicit in the agreement. They are all likely to be different!

Therefore, at whatever level you are working, you need to be aware of the full implications of an SLA, often because it is the person working at, for example, the enquiry desk, the interlibrary loans section, the search service section, or the ordering section who has the most detailed knowledge of the systems that will have to meet any agreements. For instance, it is no good agreeing to providing an interlibrary loans service that states that an item can be delivered usually within 48 hours when you know the norm is more like four days unless you pay for express delivery services that have not been costed into the agreement. In particular, you should be aware of any penalties that can be invoked if your service fails to meet standards. Your credibility, and the acceptability of your innovative ideas, will be damaged if you fail to meet your basic targets.

Features of an SLA

SLAs were first widely used to manage relationships with corporate computing sections and have a number of features that reflect their origins. They are often a feature of quality management systems, where their precision aids the process of the definition of products and services. They clarify the relationship between the supplier and the customer by setting out expectations and responsibilities, and the commitment of both parties to the agreement. Setting out in the contract the customer's responsibilities as well as the supplier's should avoid any arguments, which can arise unnecessarily, for example, when users have more details about requested documents than they actually reveal. Most information workers will have experienced the situation where a user asks vaguely for some reference, only to find that they already have all the details, but omitted to tell the information and library service! The implied suggestion is that it is up to the supplier to find the item required without further clues.

The SLA is also a planning tool for the supplier, allowing the prediction of troughs and peaks of activity. The SLA is prescriptive, but this should concern what is to be done rather than how it is to be carried out. To describe and define the required result is useful; to say how it is to be done is unnecessarily restrictive. There are often alternative and possibly better ways of achieving the end, which the supplier may be freer to implement than was the management line.

The SLA should include details of exceptions to the agreement, particularly anticipated and permissible exceptions. If a standard service is provided (which may be defined in a brochure or service statement) then the agreement need only refer to the standard terms and then list the variations, exceptions, or enhancements.

The SLA will contain elements of a number of different types of specification in a single document. These include:

➤functional specification: a definition of what the system has to achieve or do, probably expressed in terms of outputs or achievements

➤performance specification: setting levels of performance, for example by setting a minimum quota of actions to be completed in a stated time for various LIS functions ('90% of enquiries from the management floor to be answered within 60 minutes')

➤technical specification: although this is to be avoided, in practical terms it is often not possible to exclude a definition of some of the systems and services to be used ('the LIS will use the XYZ Ltd connection to Internet Services Providers Ltd for external electronic mail communications').

What SLAs do not do

SLAs need not be restrictive, although they can be and have been in practice when too little imagination is used and the agreed terms allow no freedom to develop. New models of service delivery can be established alongside and within the SLA. These have often proved to be necessary to fill in areas missed in the service definition, and partnerships have been set up with external suppliers to develop additional services or to provide investment in new areas. There should be regular SLA progress meetings in which the supplier works alongside the customer rather than in opposition: conveniently, these meetings can form part of the peer knowledge networking system which we mentioned in Chapter 6.

We have examined all aspects of service level agreements in another Library Association Publishing title, *The complete guide to preparing and implementing service level agreements*.

Whichever course is chosen by the information and library service, it is a useful exercise to have prepared a list of the services that it provides, including definitions in a glossary as necessary. Even within information and library services there is considerable confusion over the multiple meanings of words such as 'circulation', 'series', and 'copy'. Distinctions may well be lost by management staff putting together an operational requirement without the benefit of professional advice. These contract managers may rely on trade literature to guide their efforts, and it may well use different terminology, particularly in describing systems of American origin.

Terminology such as 'routing' and 'circulation' is capable of two or more interpretations. If you mean journal circulation say so; if you mean book circulation in the sense of the old-fashioned circulating library, say that. A moment's reflection will show that the document in question moves quite differently in each case, and its transits to and from the information and library service are far greater in the second instance than the first. If it is necessary to draw a distinction between 'circulation' (where the items circulated return to the information and library service) and 'distribution' (where the users retain the documents sent to them), then note that distinction in your glossary. If what you already do is not clearly defined, others are unlikely to understand how an intrapreneurial style service can improve matters for them.

Precision in such matters at the outset will save considerable problems during the performance of the SLA. Nevertheless you may well be surprised at some of the supplementary questions that this provokes. A very senior director of one organization was surprised when the distinction between distribution and circulation was explained; he appeared to have believed up until then that every item ever purchased had remained in the library, which presumably had squirrelled away every reference book the organization had bought in the past 100 years of its existence! It is well to be prepared for the ramifications of such explanations.

Putting yourself in the customer's chair

Put yourself in the customer's chair and ask what you want from the information and library services. Do you want:

➤ regular information on your main subject areas?
➤ a photocopy of the contents pages of the main journals in your subject area as soon as the journal is received?
➤ to search for yourself for information via the computerized services available on the internal network or intranet?
➤ updates on your selected subject by e-mail?

➤ to be informed when any new titles or CD-ROMs etc. arrive in the information and library service?

➤ regular update information sessions?

There may be other services that can be offered, and these should be discussed with your customers.

Quality and performance management

Quality management and performance management go hand in hand, so the intrapreneur needs to be aware of the principles of quality management systems, such as ISO 9004-2 Quality Management for Services and ISO 9001 Total Quality Management.

Some information and library services aim to have regular collection of performance measurements that give details of successes and failures.

An information and library service will need to start building its quality system and constantly review where it is going. It will need to be brutal in its appraisal of the services and systems, and strive to improve, through training of staff, through innovation, through constantly asking the questions:

➤ how are we are doing?

➤ why is this job done, need it be continued, can the need for it be avoided?

➤ how is it done, why this way, can a better way be found?

➤ when is it done, why then, can a better time be found?

➤ where is it done, why there, can a better place be found?

➤ who does this job, why is it done by them/him/her, is there someone else (inside the organization or outside) who can do this job?

➤ is this really core business?

In order to achieve the quality of services and the performance measures agreed in the SLA, customers should be aware that they too have a role to play. Customers should:

➤ be aware of what their information and library services can do

➤ identify their information problems/needs

➤ communicate these to the information and library services staff and discuss them
➤ give feedback to the information and library services
➤ keep information staff aware of their changing subject interests
➤ involve the service in projects that have information implications.

In the end it is the customer who really decides the quality, by

➤ making demands for improvements
➤ asking for services
➤ showing a willingness to cooperate.

Obtaining user feedback

Having an SLA means there can be constant user feedback. The intrapreneur may wish to set up 'focus groups', which will consist of people in an organization who are not only information seekers but are also 'movers and shakers' in their own specialism or department.

These people will know when/where shifts in demands for information are taking place and will be able to feed such changes through to the information and library services. They can also be used to pass 'quality assessments' of the standards expected to be achieved.

The intrapreneur may also wish to use a focus group to try out new services or systems. It is essential that there is a constant dialogue with the users in order to be able to set and maintain standards in information and library services.

In order to help users it is necessary to define their information needs. A user survey can be carried out – on the whole service, or on a particular service, e.g. the enquiry service, or on the circulation of journals service. Such a questionnaire can be sent to all users or a sample set of users. The questionnaire will need to ask a range of questions that will require little effort of the recipient to answer. Posing questions that require nothing more time-consuming than a box to be ticked is a positive way of ensuring that the questionnaire is returned. (So to is the offer of a prize draw – a bottle of wine can be an effective way of getting questionnaires returned). You know your customers best and you should be able to think of other ways of obtaining feedback.

vices can spread within the organization because some other staff member attended the same conference or seminar.

The information centre

However small or large a space your information centre occupies, ensure that it looks professional, is inviting and user-friendly, is well organized and provides space to sit and work with the information resources. Make sure, as part of your marketing and publicity, that the information resources are well guided, and that signs are professionally produced and can be read clearly. This is all part of the image making. Get rid of that cluttered noticeboard and ensure that returned items are filed away on a daily basis!

Defining the marketing plan

When you are defining your marketing plan decide:

➤ which services you want to promote
➤ what group(s) of people you are targetting
➤ how you are going to carry out the promotion
➤ the timescale in which to fulfil the plan
➤ the publicity vehicles to be used
➤ the budget allocation.

Promoting services

It is necessary to promote services for various reasons:

➤ they are underused
➤ staff members may not know that you have access to, or have already in-house, certain products such as CD-ROMs or specialized reference sources, or that you are able to use and have access to many of the world's databases
➤ a new project within the organization may need access to some new data sources or resources that have not previously been available
➤ the acquisition of a new in-house computerized system with which customers need to be familiarized.

Case study 6

XYZ Co information and library services have had for a period of time the Standards Infodisk CD-ROM, which contains a vast array of information on worldwide standard specifications. There are some users of this product but you know that many more could benefit from using it in their daily work.

Which group of people

You and your information colleagues use this product on a continual basis to answer the enquiries of some of the 50 staff members of the engineering group. It has become apparent that many of the remaining engineering staff members would benefit from using it. Therefore to help them become more aware of the vast range of information available, you have decided to promote the wider use of the Standards Infodisk CD. Once these staff members are proficient you can release some time for developing other services.

How are you going to carry out the promotion?

First, before any promotion takes place, you will need to ensure that you and your colleagues are well trained in all aspects of the CD to be able to pass on the knowledge and skills that are needed. You must have confident staff who are able to instruct users and answer their questions, so some investment of time will be needed before the publicity starts.

The timescale in which to fulfil the plan

Once the staff training has been completed, then you can decide how much time will be allocated to this project to be able to fulfil the marketing plan.

You know that there is a potential audience of about forty people who may all clamour at the same time for use of the CD-ROM. You will need to establish a dialogue with the head of the engineering department to discuss why you believe that marketing of the

Standards Infodisk service will benefit his staff members. Once agreement has been reached you will need to spell out how the promotion will take place.

Here you need to decide the timescale to fulfil the plan – in this case four months are allowed:

➤ Month 1
  • establish plan and discuss with the head of the engineering department.
➤ Month 2
  • start the marketing and promotion using various publicity vehicles (see below)
  • early response to the publicity.
➤ Month 3
  • further responses
  • review the plan, decide if successful, make any adjustments
  • further promotion.
➤ Month 4
  • final take-up
  • final assessment.

The publicity vehicles to be used

It is often said that in any kind of publicity you have to tell people at least three times before the message is digested, so you will have to think of packaging the message in a number of different ways. Just look at how advertisers get the message across for a food item!

You will need to decide which are the best publicity vehicles to suit your audiences. For a quick marketing and promotion task you will need to think of what is available that is not very expensive, so it will depend largely on putting the plan through the existing vehicles.

These could be:

➤ using e-mail by sending a message to each individual (success here depends on individuals actually reading their e-mail!)

75

➤ distributing a printed current awareness newsletter, which could carry an advert describing the product
➤ 'knocking on doors', meaning that you or a member of the information team would need to make an appointment with the staff member to discuss and/or demonstrate the product
➤ publicizing and hosting an open day or session by which you could invite staff into the information centre for a demonstration of the product – providing a buffet or refreshments gives people an extra incentive to take up the offer
➤ writing to or telephoning people offering to search for a particular piece of information pertinent to their current job or interests
➤ designing and publishing a brochure that can be sent to staff members.

There are other ways of publicizing the information and library service, as follows.

The training department

Working with the training department and ensuring that whenever there is an induction course for new staff members that you are allocated a slot (perhaps 30 minutes) where you can give an overview of the information and library services. And do have an information pack, which the newcomer can refer to at a later time. Look at areas of overlap between the training department's collection of books and pamphlets and your own – and help them organize their collection so you can find things when they are wanted!

Also, if your organization uses a lot of acronyms and abbreviations, consider putting together an 'Acronyms and Abbreviations Glossary'. You will be surprised how much this is appreciated.

The organization's newsletter

Take every opportunity to promote the information and library services in the newsletter by writing about new products, journals, and other items of information that should interest readers.

SDI

Selective dissemination of information means that you can select pertinent new information for an individual or a group of people working on the same project. Encourage one of the members to act as gatekeeper to the group and you will be able to use this link to publicize any further activities.

The budget allocation

What you are able to do will depend on the amount of the budget allocated to the above marketing and promotion activities. It may be possible to allocate one information staff member to these activities, so that there is some consistency in the responses to any queries which may arise from the recipients of the marketing and promotion activities. Ideally this would be a press or publicity officer. Staff time should be costed and included in the budget. In addition time may be needed to describe a product or resource, but remember that you can cut corners here by using a producer's or supplier's own brochure with some added information written by you.

Evaluation of the success of the marketing plan and publicity

You will certainly know if your marketing and promotion activities have been successful because you will have an increase in activities, not only in those aspects of the service that you have been promoting, but in general uptake on all services should increase, such as:

> - the number of quick reference enquiries
> - the number of general searches for information
> - demand for journals that are not currently taken, so an increase initially in the use of external document supply centres
> - demand for new publications
> - use of the centre itself.

You should keep statistics of the usage of each of the services, and your computerized information system should be capable of recording how often each staff member uses which service such as loans, journals, etc.

Points for reflection:

➤ What is the image of the information and library service?
➤ What is your marketing and promotion plan?
➤ Which services do you want to market?
➤ How will you promote these?
➤ How can you evaluate your success?
➤ Do you wish to allocate a percentage of the information and library services annual budget for publicity and promotion activities?

Appendix 1
Sample audit forms (see Chapter 3)

User information needs: experts

Ask the user to tick the relevant boxes

Information needs	Labour inspectorates	Research organizations	Universities	Ministries, governmental bodies	Employers	Other services	Other institutes or organizations	Worker organizations	Other
Legislation									
Codes of practice									
Technical/ health information									
Standard specifications									
Experience from abroad									
Congresses etc. abroad									
Standardized statistics									
Inventory of solutions									
Inventory of enterprises									
Literature reviews									
Journals/newsletters									
Videos									
Books, reports, pamphlets									
Computer databases/banks									
CD-ROMs									
Floppy disks									
Software programs									

How user groups currently obtain information: experts

Information needs	Labour inspectorates	Research organizations	Universities	Ministries, governmental bodies	Employers	Other services	Other institutes or organizations	Worker organizations	Other
Unions									
Universities, etc.									
Large industries									
Professional groups and their libraries, etc.									
Everyday practice									
Institutes working in prevention									
International and EU sources									
Ministries and government bodies									
Personal initiatives (e.g. private libraries)									
Personal contacts									
Congresses, seminars, etc.									

Useful means of information dissemination (on basis of users' experience and their reality): experts

Information needs	Labour inspectorates	Research organizations	Universities	Ministries, governmental bodies	Employers	Other services	Other institutes or organizations	Worker organizations	Other
Newspapers									
Journals, newsletters									
Books, reports, pamphlets, proceedings etc.									
Translation									
Technical information									
Transparencies									
Videos									
TV, radio									
Campaigns on specific issues									
Exhibitions									
Seminars, etc.									
Oral advice									
Fax									
Computer databases/banks									
CD-ROMs									
Floppy disks									
Software programs									
E-mail									

User groups' information needs: non expert/technical level

Information needs	Journalists, editors	Employers, including small and medium enterprises	Worker organizations	Ministries, governmental bodies	Other
Legislation					
Codes of practice					
Technical/health information					
New prevention methods					
Standard specifications					
Experiences abroad					
Congresses etc. abroad					
Statistics					
Inventory of solutions					
List of producers, training centres, etc.					
Literature reviews					
Journals/newsletters					
Videos					
Books, reports, pamphlets, research, etc.					
Computer databases/banks					
CD-ROMs					
Floppy disks					
Software programs					

How user groups currently obtain information: non expert/technical level

Outlets	Journalists, editors	Employers, including small and medium enterprises	Worker organizations	Ministries, governmental bodies	Other
Unions/labour centres					
Universities, etc.					
Industry					
Professional groups, etc.					
Everyday reality					
Institutes working in prevention					
International and EU sources					
Ministries and governmental bodies					
Personal initiatives e.g. private libraries					
Personal contacts					
Congresses, seminars, etc.					
Exhibitions					

Useful means of information dissemination (on the basis of users' experience and their reality): non-expert/technical level

Useful means of information dissemination	Journalists, editors	Employers, including small and medium enterprises	Worker organizations	Ministries, governmental bodies	Other
Newspapers					
Journals, newsletters					
Books, reports, pamphlets, research, etc.					
Translations					
Technical information					
Transparencies					
Videos					
Slides					
Cassette tapes					
Posters					
Seminars, etc.					
Oral/telephone requests					
Fax					
Computer databases/banks					
CD-ROMs					
Floppy disks					
Software programs					
E-mail					

User groups' information needs: technical level

Information needs	Company technicians	Employers, including small and medium enterprises	Ministries, governmental bodies	International bodies	Business and union organizations	Other
Legislation						
Codes of practice						
Technical/health information and latest developments						
Standard specifications						
Experiences abroad						
Congresses, etc.						
Standardized statistics						
Inventory of solutions						
Inventory of enterprises						
Literature reviews						
Journals/newsletters						
Videos						
Books, reports, pamphlets, research results						
Lists of labs, institutes, etc.						
Market research on relevant topics						
Computer databases/banks						
CD-ROMs						
Floppy disks						
Software programs						

How user groups currently obtain information: technical level

Outlets	Company technicians medium enterprises	Employers, including small and bodies	Ministries, governmental	International bodies organizations	Business and union	Other
Unions						
Universities, etc.						
Industry						
Professional groups and their libraries, etc.						
Everyday practice						
Institutes working in prevention						
International and EU sources						
Ministries and governmental bodies (inspectorates)						
Personal initiatives (e.g. private libraries)						
Personal contacts						
Congresses, seminars, etc.						
Newspapers						

Useful means of information dissemination (on the basis of users' experience and their reality): technical level

Useful means of information dissemination	Journalists, editors	Employers, including small and medium enterprises	Worker organizations	Ministries, governmental bodies	Other
Newspapers					
Journals, newsletters					
Books, reports, pamphlets, original, research etc.					
Translations					
Technical information					
Transparencies					
Videos					
Slides					
Competitions, prizes, etc.					
Exhibitions					
Seminars, etc.					
Oral advice					
Fax					
Computer databases/banks					
CD-ROMs					
Floppy disks					
Software programs					
E-mail					

Appendix 2
Further reading

Chapter 1 Introducing the information intrapreneur

Boyett, I. and Findlay, D., 'The emergence of the educational entrepreneur', *Long Range Planning*, 26, 1993, 114–22.

Boyett, I., 'The public sector entrepreneur - a definition', *International journal of public sector management*, **9** (2), 1996, 36–51.

Cantillon, R., *Essai sur la nature du commerce en generale*, ed. by H. Higgs, London, Macmillan, 1931.

Leadbeater, C., *The rise of the social entrepreneur*, London, Demos, 1996.

Leadbeater, C., 'Innovation and risk taking that break free of bureaucracy', *Financial Times*, 28 April 1998, 16.

Leadbeater, C. and Goss, S., *Civic entrepreneur*, London, Demos, with the Public Management Foundation, 1998.

Library and Information Commission, *New library: the people's network*, 1997.
(Available online at <http://www.ukoln.ac.uk/services/lic/newlibrary/>.)

Marshall, Joanne G., *The impact of information services on decision making: some lessons from the financial & healthcare sectors*, London, British Library Research and Development Department, 1993. (Information policy briefings, 1).

Marshall, Joanne G., *The impact of the special library on corporate decision-making*, Washington, D.C., Special Libraries Association, 1993.

Pinchot, G., *Intrapreneuring: why you don't have to leave the corporation to become an entrepreneur*, New York, Harper & Row, 1985.

Say, J. B., *Treatise on political economy*, Philadelphia, John Grigg, 1827.

The impact of information on decision-making in Government: a half-day seminar for chief and senior librarians in government departments and agencies organized by TFPL Ltd and the Circle of State Librarians, London, 3 October 1996. [unpublished presentations]

White, H. S., *Managing the special library*, White Plains, N. J., Scarecrow, 1986.

National and international information policies

Better government, London, The Stationery Office, 1998. [forthcoming command paper].

Chancellor of the Duchy of Lancaster, United Kingdom, *Government.direct: a prospectus for the electronic delivery of government services*, (Cm 3438), London, The Stationery Office, 1996.

High Level Group on the Information Society, *Europe and the global information society: recommendations to the European Council*, chairman, Martin Bangemann, Brussels, The Group, 1994.
(Available at <http://www.ispo.cec.be/infosoc/backg/bangeman.html>)

Martin-Lalande, P., *Internet, un vrai défi pour la France: rapport au Premier Ministre*, Paris, La Documentation Française, 1998.
(Available at <http://www.premier-ministre.gouv.fr/>.)

Ministry of information and communication, South Korea, *White paper*, Seoul, Ministry of Information and Communication, 1997.
(Available at <http://www.mic.go.kr/english/paper>.) See particularly section 6, 'Preparing for the information society'.

Ministry of transport and communications, Norway, *Den norske IT-veiens: bit for bit*, Oslo, ODIN, 1996. Also available in English as *The Norwegian way to the information society: bit by bit: report from the State Secretary, Committee for IT*.
(Available at <http://odin.dep.no/it/it-way>.)

National Computer Board, Singapore, *IT 2000: a vision of an intelligent island*, Singapore, NCB, 1997.
(Available at <http://www.ncb.gov.sg/ncb/vision.asp>.)

Service d'Information du Gouvernement, France, *Préparer l'entrée de la France dans la société de l'information/programme d'action gouvernemental*, Paris, La Documentation Française, 1998.

Websites

European Commission DG XIII/E, Telematics Applications Programme Information Engineering: <http://www.echo.lu/ie/en/iehome.html>.

UK government information: <http://www.direct.access.gov.uk>

The website for case study 2 (Chapter 1), the RCRA Library is <http:/www.benton.org/Practice/Lessons/rcra.html>

Chapter 2 The organization and the information intrapreneur

Abell, A., 'So you want to be a CKO too …', *Library and information appointments*, 10 April 1998, 133–4.

Aslib, *Handbook of special librarianship and information work*, ed. A. Scammell, 7th edn, London, 1997.

Corrall, S., *Strategic planning for library and information services*, London, Aslib, 1994.

Davenport, T. and Prusak, L., *Working knowledge: how organizations manage what they know*, USA, Harvard Business School Press, 1998.

Library Association, *Developing business/service plans for a competitive future: LA training package*, London, Library Association Publishing, 1997.

Newsome, C., 'Wellcome information for better business', *Information week*, 29, 13–26 May 1998, 22–4.

Nonaka, I. and Takeuchi, H., *The knowledge creating company*, Oxford, *Oxford* University Press, 1995.

Slater, M., *The neglected resource: non-usage of library–information services in industry and commerce*, London, Aslib, 1981.

Wyllie, J., 'The need for business information refineries', *Aslib proceedings*, **45** (4), April 1993, 97–102.

Chapter 3 The internal information audit

Burk, C. F., Jr. and Horton, F. W., Jr. *InfoMap: the complete guide to discovering corporate information resources*, Prentice-Hall, 1988.
(Available from Information Management Press, Inc., PO Box 19166, Washington, DC 20036, USA.)

Hildebrand, C., 'Information mapping: guiding principles', *CIO: the magazine for information executives*, **8** (18), July 1995, 60–4.

Horton, F. W., Jr., 'Infomapping', *The electronic library*, **9** (1), February 1991, 17–19.

Horton, F. W., Jr., *The information management workbook: IRM made simple*, rev. and updated 3rd edn, 1983, Washington, DC, Information Management Press, Inc., PO Box 19166.

Horton, F. W., Jr., 'Mapping corporate information resources', *International journal of information management*, **8**, 1988, 249–54; 9, 1989,19–24; 9, 1989, 91–95.

Owen, T., *Success at the enquiry desk*, 3rd edn, London, Library Association Publishing, 1998.

Reuters, *Dying for information*, London, 1997.

Chapter 4 Keeping one step ahead of the customers

Morris, B., *First steps in management*, London, Library Association Publishing, 1996.

Owen, T., *Success at the enquiry desk*, 3rd edn, London, Library Association Publishing, 1998.

See also reading list for Chapter 8.

Chapter 5 Delivering innovative services

Bertot, J. C. and McClure, C. R., *Policy issues and strategies affecting public libraries in the national networked environment: moving beyond connectivity*, Washington, US National Commission on Libraries and Information Science, 1997.
(Available at <http://www.nclis.gov>.)

Department for Education and Employment, UK, *The learning age: a renaissance for a new Britain*, (Cm 3790), London, The Stationery Office, 1998.
(Available at <http://www.lifelonglearning.co.uk/greenpaper/index. htm>.)

International Business Machines, Inc., *The net result: social inclusion in the information society. Report of the National Working Party on Social Inclusion (INSINC)*, London, IBM United Kingdom Ltd, 1997.
(Available at <http://www.uk.ibm.com/comm/community/uk117.html>.)

Kirby, J. and others, *Empowering the information user*, London, Library Association Publishing, 1997.

Ormes, S., and Dempsey, L. (eds.), *The Internet, networking and the public library*, London, Library Association Publishing, 1997.

See also Library and Information Commission, *New library : the people's network* (reference in list for Chapter 1)

Websites

Baltimore County Public Library Senior Centre: <http://www.bcpl.lib. md.us/centers/senior/senior.html>.

Comhairle nan Eilean Siar (formerly Western Isles council) Gateway Project, The Virtual Mitchell: <http://www.ariadne.ac.uk/issue14/news/#scottish>.
Investors in people: <http://www.iipuk.co.uk>.
Queens Library (InfolinQ, Las paginas en español): <http://www.queens.lib.ny.us/>.
Treasure Island (UKOLN): <http://www.ukoln.ac.uk/services/treasure/>.

Chapter 6 Building the perfect team

Abell, A., *The information professional of the 21st century*, London, TFPL, 1997.
Bluck, R., *Team management*, London, Library Association Publishing, 1996.
Circle of State Librarians, *Time for change: threat or opportunity?* ed. P. Ryan, London, 1997. Distributed by The Stationery Office.
Lyon, J., 'Personal development: understanding knowledge', *Information world review*, May 1997, 24–5.
Pantry, S., 'Whither the information professional? Challenges and opportunities: the cultivation of information professional for the new Millennium', Presented at the ASLIB Electronics and Multimedia Groups Annual Conference, 14–16 May 1997, *Aslib proceedings*, **49** (6), June 1997,170–2.

Chapter 7 Setting and maintaining standards

Abbott, C., *Performance measurement in library and information services*, London, Aslib, 1994.
Bennett, D., *Quality assurance: two day course 26–27 June 1991*, London, Aslib, 1991.
Brockman, J. (ed.), *Quality management and benchmaking in the information sector: results of recent research* (British Library Research and Innovation Report 47), London, Bowker-Saur, 1997.
European Commission, DG XIII-E3, *Library performance indicators and library management tools*, by Suzanne Ward and others, Luxembourg, Office for Official Publications of the European Communities, 1995.
Griffiths, J.-M. and King, D. W., *A manual on the evaluation of information centers and services (manuel pour l'évaluation des centres et services d'information)*, (AGARDograph, 310), Paris, AGARD, 1991.

See also Office of Arts and Libraries, below.

Laamanen, I., 'Quality management in the information service centre of the FIOH', in *Health information management: what strategies?*, ed. by S. Bakker, The Netherlands, Kluwer Academic, 1997, 57–60.

Library Association, *Delivering quality library and information services: LA training package*, London, Library Association Publishing, 1996.

MacLachlan, L., *Making project management work for you*, London, Library Association Publishing, 1996.

Martin, D., *Total quality management*, (Library and Information Briefings 45), London, LITC, 1993.

Masterton, A. *Getting results with time management*, London, Library Association Publishing, 1997.

Office of Arts and Libraries, *Keys to success: performance indicators for public libraries* (Library information series, 18), London, HMSO, 1990.

A manual of performance measures and indicators developed by King Research Ltd, this is an abridged version of Griffiths and King, above.

Pantry, S. and Griffiths, P., *The complete guide to service level agreements*, London, Library Association Publishing, 1997.

Chapter 8 Marketing and promotion

Bates, M. E., 'Avoiding the ax: how to keep from being downsized or out-sourced', *Information outlook*, October 1997, 18–21.

Coote, H. and Batchelor, B., *How to market your library service effectively*, 2nd edn, London. Aslib, 1998.

Hamilton, F., *Infopromotion*, London, Gower, 1990.

Hart, K., *Marketing your information services*, London, Library Association Publishing, 1998.

Library Association, *Marketing library and information services: LA training package*, London, Library Association Publishing, 1997.

De Sáez, E. E, *Marketing concepts for libraries an information services*, London, Library Association Publishing, 1993.

Schmidt, J. *Marketing the modern information center: a guide to intrapreneurship for the information manager*, New York, Find/SVP, 1987.

Other material

Allen, B., *InfoMapper instructor's guide*, for use with InfoMapper software (but sold separately), Information Management Press, Inc., PO Box 19166, Washington, DC 20036, USA.

Covey, S. R., *The seven habits of highly successful people: restoring the character ethic*, USA, Simon & Schuster, 1989.

Journal of knowledge management.

Lannon, R., *InfoMapper project manager's guide*, for use with InfoMapper software (but sold separately), Information Management Press, Inc., PO Box 19166, Washington, DC 20036, USA.

Software

InfoMapper software package, IBM Compatible Standalone PC Version (Release 1.2 Mod. 1), with user manual. LAN also available, as well as French, Spanish, and German language IBM-compatible PC versions. Information Management Press, Inc., PO Box 19166, Washington, DC 20036, USA.

Web-based information

Pinchot and Company
<http://www.pinchot.com>

The web site for Gifford and Elizabeth Pinchot's company contains key texts on intrapreneurship, including 'The intrapreneur's ten commandments'.

Index

audit *see* information audit

case studies   8, 10, 37, 38, 74
champions   15
communication   40, 72
computer-based information systems
    31
contracting out   8
critical success factors   43
current awareness services   38
customers *see also* users   33, 36
    keeping ahead of   43

experts   31

information
    access   46–9; for minorities   47,
        49; in rural areas   48; for senior
        citizens   48–9
    audit   22, 28; forms   Appendix 1
    external sources   31
    needs   22, 29
    service definitions   26
    scientists *see* librarians and
        information scientists
    users   17, 30, 33, 68;
        responsibilities of   43
innovation   45–53
intrapreneur
    characteristics of   8, 56
    defined   3
    information intrapreneur   x, 4
    introducing   1–10

Pinchot's ten commandments   56

knowledge management   18–21

lessons learned programmes   10
librarians and information
    scientists
    coaching skills   50
    core skills   52, 55
    image   71, 73
    presentation skills   40
    skills convergence   59
lifelong learning   49

marketing
    information services   42, 70
    plans   73, 77

organizations   12
    management   24, 57
    peer networks in   58
    publications   13, 17, 60
    staff   14

partnerships   52
performance measures   67
promotion 70
publicity vehicles   75

quality 39, 67

rising stars   15

service level agreements   63
services
    innovative   45
    practical problems   51
    promotion   73
staff
    knowledge and skills   52, 55
    management   57

    team 54
    updating 35
standards 61

teams 54
technology 45–8; and skills conver-
    gence 59
telecommunications and networks
    27, 31
training
  computer-assisted 50

departments 39, 76

users
  established 14
  expectations 36
  feedback 68
  potential 14
  requirements 33
  responsibilities of 43
  support from 15, 57
  types of 29